# SP**EAKING** WITH

# **E**

# BETTERWAY BOOKS
## CINCINNATI, OHIO

97  96  95  94  93      5  4  3

**Library of Congress Cataloging in Publication Data**

Vassallo, Wanda
    Speaking with confidence : a guidebook for public speakers / Wanda Vassallo.
       p. cm.
    Includes bibliographical references.
    ISBN 1-55870-147-8
    1. Public speaking. I. Title.
    PN4121.V37    1990
    808.5'1 — dc20                     89-29921
                                           CIP

Cover design by Deborah B. Chappell
Typography by Park Lane Associates.

*For Richard and Laurie*

*who grew up in the audience and were often part of the act*

# Acknowledgments

*With special thanks to my AAA friends:*

*Larry Ascough, my mentor in the field of communications;*

*Dean Angel, communicator extraordinary;*

*Richard M. Adams, M.D., for sharing his expertise*
*on the physiological aspects of public speaking.*

# Contents

# Foreword

As an apprentice in the craft of speech making, I feel a little presumptuous in introducing *Speaking with Confidence*, a book by a master in the field. Wanda Vassallo knows everything there is to know on the subject, because she has done it all.

She is an outstanding speaker herself. She has written literally thousands of speeches, including most of the ones I gave during my ten years as superintendent of the Dallas Independent School District. She has scripted and produced television programs; hosted radio shows; taught speech, drama, and public speaking; and has written and produced newsletters, reports, and other publications. She is also a singer, an ordained minister, and appears before church and civic groups as Flutter the Clown.

And now she has written this book.

Let me say that it is an extraordinary piece of work. For one thing, it is the most thorough treatment of the subject I have ever seen. For instance, Wanda knows that there are important things a good speaker should do even before stepping up to a podium. She treats in detail such diverse matters as how to overcome stage fright, how to sit in your chair before you are introduced, how to size up your audience before you prepare your speech, how to find material, even what physical exercises to practice. These are among the most important lessons to learn in establishing and maintaining confidence; yet too many books on the subject begin with the speaker standing in front of the microphone, mouth open, about to address the audience.

Then, too, Wanda's book is specific and concrete in many areas where other treatments are frustratingly generalized and vague. For example, she offers: specific guidance on what to wear and what to avoid; specific ways to loosen up and make your gestures more effective and more relevant to your point; twenty-seven specific things the speaker can do to get and keep the audience's attention; and even a specific list of things that turn listeners off. I was particularly gratified to find not only a catalog of possible openings for speeches, but also an example of each, taken from a well-known or successful presentation.

On the surface this book is light reading. It is witty. It is entertaining. And it is full of factual information organized in easily recognizable categories. But it is really a more serious study than it seems on the surface, because the subject itself is more important than most people realize. In the past twenty-five years we have become a nation of teachers and communicators, in large measure because more and more we have acquired specialized information from which others can benefit.

For example, the business world increasingly asks its employees to make public appearances in order to share information about new goods and services, the latest technology, or a recently developed expertise. Not only are CEOs required to make speeches on a regular basis, but also executives and heads of research and development. And, of course, sales personnel are always making presentations to create new accounts and sell new items in their line. As American business has grown more complex and more versatile, it has also demanded more of those who enter its ranks; and public speaking is often cited as an essential skill in considering people for hiring or promotion.

But even those who are not in business are often required to make presentations before large bodies—church groups, professional organizations, political gatherings. Few people these days make it through adult life without having to come before an audience of total strangers, speech in hand, and face a moment when the room is silent and everyone turns expectantly, eyes alert, ready to be enlightened and entertained. The chances are you won't escape that moment any more than I have. (In fact, children begin their careers as public speakers during show-and-tell in the first grade.)

But it needn't be a terrifying experience or even an unpleasant one. In accepting such challenges most of us discover that we have a greater potential for self-expression than we were previously aware of and that this untapped human potential can only be fully realized if we are willing to make sacrifices in order to be better and to take chances in order to reach out to others.

Sacrifices are necessary when you strive to be the best you can in that particular area or field. As for taking chances, any new encounter with another human being involves risks, since you never know whether you are meeting a lifelong friend or a potentially dangerous enemy. But when you are dealing with an audience, your potential for making new friends or enemies is multiplied tenfold, a hundredfold, or a thousandfold, depending on the size of the crowd. For some people this thought is too disturbing to contemplate. When you have finished Wanda Vassallo's book, however, you will regard it as something to anticipate with confidence and optimism.

Because, though speech making is a complicated and demanding subject, Wanda makes it much easier and more fun in *Speaking with Confidence*. With her guidance, the sacrifices become enjoyable recreation and the chances become adventures. Mark Twain once said that it took him at least two weeks to prepare an impromptu speech. If he had read Wanda's book he could probably have done it in a couple of days.

And while you won't master public speaking in that amount of time, I'm willing to bet that Wanda will have you up on a platform almost immediately, addressing your audience with greater confidence, and sitting down to genuine applause.

Linus Wright
Former Under Secretary,
U.S. Department of Education

# *Preview*

## HUH? WHAT DID YOU SAY?

Do you suffer from logophobia or embolalia?

No, they're not diseases. But they can make your speech turn limpid and pale.

Logophobia is the fear of speaking—a much more dignified-sounding malady than stage fright, don't you think?

Embolalia is the word for speech fillers like . . . y'know . . . er . . . um . . . o.k. . . . right? Y'know what I mean?

Never fear. Anaphora and videocybernetics can help you out as a speaker.

Anaphora—the repetition of a word or phrase at the beginning of successive sentences or paragraphs—is the hallmark of such stirring oratory as Martin Luther King's "I Have a Dream" and John F. Kennedy's "Let Them Come to Berlin."

Videocybernetics—training and coaching with video feedback—are powerful tools for improving your skills as a speaker.

Since many speeches are delivered in an auditorium, it's also interesting to note that the word auditorium is derived from two Latin words:

audio—TO HEAR

taurus—THE BULL

# 1

## *Making Friends with Your Worst Enemy: You!*

Consider: The comic strip character Pogo waxed eloquently philosophical when he said, "We have met the enemy, and it is us."[1]

While his words of wisdom could easily relate to many areas of living, certainly one of the most appropriate applications would have to be in the challenging area of speaking before an audience. There is no doubt that the worst enemy most of us have as public speakers is ourselves.

There are many skills to conquer in becoming an effective speaker, but probably the biggest conquest that has to be made is the person we see in the mirror each morning. "Public Speaking and Other Coronary Threats" was the title used for an article by Max D. Isaacson, vice president of Maxmillan Oil Co.[2] While it is a whimsically amusing title, most people find getting up before an audience anything but a laughing matter.

In fact, speaking before a group was listed as the number one fear of U.S. inhabitants who ranked fourteen common fears. Fear of death was number seven on the list.[3] From this, we can logically conclude that most people would rather die than get up and speak. Also, consider the fact that speaking before a group is one of the five highest stress factors.

Someone has said, "When it comes to public speaking, many are called, but few want to get up." Most of us can relate to this observation:

"The brain is a remarkable thing. It starts to function the instant you are born and doesn't stop until the moment you get up to speak."[4]

"All the world's a stage," wrote Shakespeare, who might well have added, ". . . and every player on it has stage fright."

A marvelous story about stage fright involves an incident that supposedly took place in the days of the Roman Empire during a circus in the Coliseum. It seems that a Christian was thrown to a hungry lion. As the spectators cheered, the wild beast pounced. But the Christian quickly whispered something in the lion's ear and the beast backed away in terror. After this happened several times, the emperor sent a centurion to find out what magic spell could make ferocious lions cower in fear. A few minutes later the guard returned and said, "The Christian whispers in the lion's ear, 'After dinner you'll be required to say a few words.'"[5]

Remember the words of E. Hubbard: "The greatest mistake you can make in life is to be continually fearing you will make one."[6] So while getting up in front of an audience is definitely a high risk, stressful situation, speaking effectively and moving and influencing listeners is definitely one of the most exhilarating and satisfying adventures a person can experience.

## HOW IMPORTANT IS COMMUNICATING EFFECTIVELY?

Consider: A recent survey showed that the number one job of people in business is to communicate successfully. Those who make the corporate wheels go round, including company presidents and chairmen of the board, spend the average day this way: 45 percent, listening; 32 percent, speaking; 14 percent, reading; and 9 percent, writing.[7]

Research reveals that 80 percent of the average person's waking hours is spent communicating in one form or another.[8]

Daniel Webster said: "If all my possessions were taken from me with one exception, I would choose to keep the power of speech, for by it I would soon regain the rest."[9]

It was the renowned psychologist Sigmund Freud who observed: "Words call forth emotions and are universally the means by which we influence our fellow creatures . . . by words, one of us can give to another the greatest happiness or bring about utter despair."[10]

"Which courses best prepare one for business leadership?" This was the question posed by the University of Michigan graduate school to 1,158 newly promoted top executives. Business communication was the most common response with 71.4 percent rating it as very important. Finance was the second highest with 64.7 percent.[11]

The eminent Dale Carnegie said: "Every activity of our lives is communication of a sort, but it is through speech that man asserts his distinctiveness . . . that he best expresses his own individuality, his essence."[12]

And Shakespeare had something to say in *King Lear* on the subject too: "Mend your speech a little, lest it may mar your fortunes."

"In my library are about a thousand volumes of biography. A rough calculation indicates that more of these deal with men who have talked themselves upward than with all the scientists, writers, saints and doers combined. Talkers have always ruled. They will continue to rule. The smart thing is to join them."[13]
—Congressman Bruce Barton

## COPING WITH STAGE FRIGHT

Consider: Everyone has the problem of learning to handle nervousness, the jitters, stage fright—whatever you want to call it. Everyone gets butterflies in the stomach. The trick is to train them to fly in formation.

Even seasoned speakers and performers admit to nervousness. Theatrical immortal Otis Skinner comforted his daughter Cornelia with this insight: "I have been in the theater for 50 years and I've never outgrown it. Any actor who claims he is immune to stage fright is either lying, or else he's no actor."[14]

So while stage fright isn't funny, it is normal, natural, and even helpful—once you learn to use it to your advantage instead of your destruction. In fact, if you ever get over that feeling of nervousness and anticipation as a speaker, you'll probably be one of two things—dead or lousy.

What happens to us when we have stage fright is the same fight-or-flight syndrome the caveman experienced when he found himself in a life or death situation. Adrenaline is released into the system as a result of physical or emotional stress, causing extra activation of the body. Some of the bodily reactions are: an increase in heart rate, a more rapid respiratory rate, more oxygen to all tissues, increased mental activity, and increased muscle strength. These changes enable the person to run faster and to have much greater strength.

A few years ago a woman came upon the scene of an accident near Beaumont, Texas. A child was pinned under the wheel of a truck. The driver was injured, and there was no one else in sight. The woman jumped out of her car, ran to the truck and lifted it, freeing the child. Later, after the child and the driver had been taken to the hospital, she went over to the truck and could not budge it. Only the extreme stress of seeing a child under the truck's wheel activated the strength she needed.

Once we learn to use our souped-up bodies to advantage, we can do a better job than we normally could. We can capitalize on the increased energy. Our brains will be sharper; our thinking clearer. And there are definite steps we can take to cope with any negative changes brought about when our bodies get ready to fight or flee.

The shakes, the hot and cold flashes, the nausea, the damp palms, the cold sweat dripping down the ribs, the dry throat can all be controlled and conquered.

Last, but not least, do some relaxation exercises. Here are some you probably will find helpful.

*The Spaghetti Exercise:* Picture yourself as a piece of uncooked spaghetti that is slowly dropped, feet first in boiling water. Feel your toes get soft, your feet, your ankles, the calves of your legs, all the way up to the top of your head.

***Body Relaxation:*** Dr. Boino Kiveloff of the New York Infirmary/Beekman Downtown Hospital has developed a daily exercise to help keep one's blood pressure at a healthy level.[17] He recommends doing it three times daily, but it can help a speaker right before a speaking engagement also.

Steal away to a quiet corner, restroom, etc., where you can be alone for a few minutes.

1. Stand in a comfortable position with your arms hanging loose at your sides. Relax your elbows and knees and keep your hands unclenched.

2. Tighten every muscle in your body, either in unison or by groups. Still tensed, breathe normally and count aloud to six.
3. Relax your muscles and rest briefly.
4. Repeat the exercise two more times.

*Progressive Relaxation Exercise:* The sixteen steps in this exercise require you to tense each muscle group for six seconds and then completely relax them for thirty seconds.

Muscle Group

1. Dominant hand
2. Dominant upper arm
3. Non-dominant hand
4. Non-dominant upper arm
5. Forehead
6. Eyes and nose
7. Mouth and jaw
8. Neck and throat
9. Upper back
10. Stomach
11. Dominant upper leg
12. Dominant lower leg
13. Dominant foot
14. Non-dominant upper leg
15. Non-dominant lower leg
16. Non-dominant foot

*Other Relaxation Exercises:*

1. Upper arm. Press your elbow down and pull toward your body for six seconds, then relax thirty seconds.
2. Forehead. Wrinkle your brow into a frown. Relax.
3. Mouth and jaw. Clench your jaw. Relax.
4. Neck and throat. Press your head back against the chair. Relax.
5. Upper back. Pull your shoulders up and forward. Relax.
6. Stomach. Pull your stomach in as far as you can, or push it out. Relax.
7. Upper leg. Lift your leg very slightly. Relax.
8. Lower leg. Point your toes away from your head. Relax.

## THIRTEEN WAYS TO OVERCOME STAGE FRIGHT

1.   Dress comfortably in clothes you like and feel good in. It's important to you psychologically to feel confident of the way you look. As someone said: "You can't lead a cavalry charge if you think you look funny sitting on a horse."[15] You need to think you look like a seasoned speaker.

2.   Be well-prepared. Don't wait until the last minute to put your speech together. Rehearse several times. Program your mind with your material to the point that you can give your speech regardless of what might happen.

3.   Concentrate on your message. When you believe you have something important to share with your audience, it's easy to get excited about what you're going to tell them. When you focus on your message, you likely will forget about yourself. As Lady Bird Johnson observed: "The way you overcome shyness is to become so wrapped up in something, you forget to be afraid."[16]

4.   Take several deep breaths. The increased respiratory rate we usually experience as a result of stage fright can cause lots of problems. Not only do we run out of breath every few words, we also lack the support necessary for good vocal production. Breathing deeply breaks this cycle and has a calming effect. A good approach is to breathe from the diaphragm in on a count of four, hold your breath four counts and breathe out on the word "easy." This can be done while you are seated in front of an auditorium full of people.

5.   Move around. This releases nervous energy and restores a feeling of calm. If you are waiting in the wings to go on, take some large, brisk steps and flail your arms around. If you're seated on the dais, of course, you can't move much, but you can take advantage of your walk to the speaker's stand. But what if suddenly you start getting nervous in the middle of your speech? Find an excuse to make large arm gestures, move away from the lectern, sip a glass of water. If you're trapped at the speaker's stand by a mike you can't move, ask a rhetorical question and move while you're giving the audience time to think of the answer.

6.   Picture yourself as doing well. Use positive mental imaging. See yourself in your mind's eye being introduced,

walking to the speaker's stand, speaking to a warm, responsive audience. See how well you're doing. Hear your words flowing without hesitation. Hear the laughter of the audience, the enthusiastic applause after you are finished. See yourself as successful and run several replays of your success. Many top athletes use this positive mental imaging technique and swear by its effectiveness.

7. Make no negative confession. Whatever you do, don't say, "I know I'm going to blow it," or "I'm so nervous, I'll never get through this speech." Thinking that way is bad enough, but there's something about saying negative things about yourself that feeds your fears and makes them turn into horrible monsters.

8. Gain confidence by doing. Practice makes perfect and success builds on success.

9. Remember, your audience is made up of people just like you. They want you to do well. They don't want their time to be wasted by a lousy, boring speaker. An ill-at-ease speaker makes the listener ill-at-ease and embarrassed, too.

10. Remember an occasion when you did a really super terrific job as a speaker and relive it—several times.

11. Come to terms with the fact that if you are going to be a speaker, you're going to make mistakes—just as you will if you type or do anything else. But a mistake needn't be fatal. If you learn to laugh it off and let your audience enjoy it with you, it can become a bridge to better rapport.

12. Pick out friendly faces and make eye contact with them. An encouraging expression on a listener's face can do wonders to promote confidence. Don't look at someone with folded arms, a crabby look, or fidgety movements.

13. Cooperate with your body. This includes getting enough rest the night before so your energy peak will be at a high level. It also means eating sensibly. Eating a huge meal just before speaking is asking for problems. While the effect of different foods varies with the individual, most speakers would do well to avoid sugar-laden foods, too much caffeine, and all alcoholic beverages. For most people, a smaller-than-usual meal of high protein foods is a safe bet.

## "I'M SORRY, IN FACT, I'M THE SORRIEST . . ."

Consider: When tempted to apologize, don't! If you're a flop as a speaker, the audience will find out soon enough. Besides, if you don't tell them, they may never know.

Think about your reaction to these types of apologies from a speaker.

"Please forgive me. I'm really nervous." (Listener's reaction: "He does look nervous. Even his hands are shaking. Boy, is he ever making me uncomfortable.") (Speaker's reaction: "I'm even more nervous than I thought I was.")

"I'm really sorry, but I just didn't have time to prepare this speech the way I really wanted to." (Listener's reaction: "Thanks a lot for wasting my valuable time. Ho hum!") (Speaker's reaction: "This is really going to be a bummer. I'll just have to fumble through.")

"I don't know why I was asked to speak on this subject. There are a lot of people who know more about it than I do." (Listener's reaction: "Is this ever going to be a drag . . . one long bore.") (Speaker's reaction: "I really feel inadequate and unsure of myself.")

"I'm really not much of a speaker." (Listener's reaction: "Well, that's obvious without saying.") (Speaker's reaction: "I just hope I can make it through.")

As a speaker, remove the word "sorry" from your vocabulary . . . except in a couple of instances.

If you are unavoidably late and keep the audience waiting, you owe them an apology.

If the audience is uncomfortable and the problem cannot be corrected, you need to express concern for their comfort and well-being.

But what if something happens you just can't ignore? Say, for example, you are walking to the lectern with great poise and confidence, trip over the mike cord and fall flat on your face. What do you do then?

Rather than getting all embarrassed, turn the incident into an asset by getting your audience to laugh with you. Say something like, "Well, my speech teacher told me to get the audience's attention, but this is ridiculous," or "My pastor said I should be humble, but maybe I carried it  a little too far this time." Let the audience know it's o.k. to laugh. Otherwise, they'll be embarrassed if they did laugh, and embarrassed for you.

But don't yield to the temptation to apologize. You'll be sorry if you do!

## KEEP ON KEEPING ON

Consider: There's an old Spanish saying that goes "Ay Jalisco! No te rajes!" While something is lost in the translation, this rallying cry, basically, means, "Don't give up. Keep on keeping on!"

That would be a good motto for all of us who are trying to master the fine art of public speaking. No one is born a good speaker. It is a skill. And, like any other skill, to be mastered it must be practiced correctly until it becomes second nature to do it right. Then you can forget about the mechanics and just do it.

But in between beginning to speak and mastery, realistically you must expect to go through a learning process that is sometimes painful and discouraging. After all, how many times did you fall down before you learned to walk? Did you make a home run the first time you swung a baseball bat? Did you start out typing eighty words a minute with no errors? Every skill requires time, effort, practice, and persistence.

A reporter said to George Bernard Shaw one day, "You have a marvelous gift for oratory. How did you develop it?" Shaw replied, "I learned to speak as men learn to skate or cycle—by doggedly making a fool of myself until I got used to it."[18]

As Ralph Waldo Emerson pointed out, "All the great speakers were bad speakers at first."[19]

Someone has said, "Genius is the capacity for taking infinite pains."

After a brilliant piano concert capped by thunderous applause, the Queen of England said to the artist, "Mr. Paderewski, you are a genius." Bowing gravely, Paderewski replied, "Before I became a genius, your Majesty, I was a drudge."[20]

All of us have to be drudges—to risk failure—before we can become geniuses. But remember, you never fail until you stop trying.

Winston Churchill, considered one of history's most eloquent orators, didn't give up.

James C. Humes says, ". . . the man who was to become the 'speaker of the century' only became so after years of practice and persevering to surmount various handicaps. Churchill was hardly destined to be an orator. He had little of the God-given talents for forensic brilliance. He was born with a congenital lisp and stammer. His voice lacked the rich resonance of the platform speaker and his five-foot hunched frame was hardly an imposing presence." He "fainted dead away when he first spoke in Parliament." Even though Churchill had little going for him, "in his command of the English language, he commanded the destiny of free men. Through his mastery of the tongue, he rose in Parliament to prime minister and eventually saved the West."[21]

He knew that success comes in cans, failure in can'ts. He also realized that he didn't have to possess the oratorical powers of Cicero to be persuasive.

John F. Kennedy had a heavy New England accent. Eleanor Roosevelt's voice was not the most pleasant by anyone's standard. Dwight Eisenhower spoke in a halting monotone. Still their words swayed millions.

Don't dwell on your limitations. Do the most with what you have. Next time you're asked how to spell success, answer p-e-r-s-e-v-e-r-a-n-c-e.

Shakespeare's Macbeth had some good advice for public speakers. He said you've got to "screw your courage to the sticking place."

Joe Powell made a thought-provoking statement about the importance of perseverance. He said: "Learning to speak effectively is much easier than learning to be a parachute jumper. When learning to speak, you don't have to succeed every time you try. You just have to keep trying."[22]

And remember, the dictionary is the only place where "success" comes before "work," and by perseverance, the snail reached the ark.[23]

# 2

# *Presenting Yourself as a Speaker*

Consider: In the first four minutes, the speaker is either received or rejected by the audience.

We gather information . . .

87 percent by sight

7 percent by hearing

3.5 percent by smell

1.5 percent by touch

1 percent by taste

So what your audience sees is vitally important. Listeners need visual stimulation—a point of activity to focus on. Gestures, body language, appearance, eye contact, posture and facial animation are vitally important in addition to other visual stimuli.

The average person speaks at about 125 words per minute. The average person thinks at a rate nearly four times faster.[1] We say that our minds wander, but actually they gallop ahead of the speaker like a runaway race horse. Speakers have to do everything possible to rivet the listener's attention.

Because of TV the average person's attention span is now said to be only about seven minutes. Then it's time for the commercial . . . to run to the fridge, etc. A speaker needs a variety of pace and activities to overcome this effect on the avid TV viewer.

These facts point up the importance of making sure your listeners' eyes have pleasant, positive stimuli to keep them interested enough to listen to your message.

# APPEARANCE

Consider: How you look initially determines how willing people will be to listen to you.

As a speaker, think of *yourself* as a visual. That's what you become when you appear before an audience. Your manner of dress and attention to small details of grooming make an indelible impression about your message and the organization you represent . . . before you ever open your mouth.

These are some important areas to keep in mind.

Simplicity should be the keynote. Solid colors are safest, preferably not dazzlingly bright for the primary costume color. Any patterns should be small and rather subdued. Bold patterns can be distracting, even dizzying—especially in the case of a speaker who moves around a great deal.

Formality in dress should be at the top level of your audience or one notch above. A certain level of formality in dress projects authority and credibility as a speaker. However, a negative effect can be the result if a speaker is really overdressed for the occasion, e.g., an executive who shows up in a three-piece suit to speak at a lake retreat where everyone is wearing jeans or for a hard-hat crew of construction workers.

Comfort in dress is important. A speaking engagement is not the time to break in a new pair of shoes. Cramped, aching feet usually result eventually in a pained expression on the face. Clothing should be unrestrictive and should permit absolute freedom of movement. This is especially important to consider in relation to making gestures.

Dress for confidence. Wear something you really like and feel that you look your very best in. While a new outfit often gives a person a psychological lift, it is probably safer to select something you're used to and that feels a part of you. At least give a new wardrobe piece a trial run to be sure everything works and fits properly before wearing it on the podium.

Wear a little lighter weight clothing than you normally would. Public speaking is hard work and usually results in a rise in body temperature. You also may want to consider dressing in layers, so that you will have a removable outer garment.

Be sure the clothes you select to wear will remain as crisp looking when the time comes to speak as they were when you left for your speaking engagement. Some fabrics simply do not hold a crease or press as well as others.

Avoid dangling or large pieces of jewelry. Not only can they be distracting, they can also be very tempting for the speaker to play with—which is even more distracting. Don't wear anything you might unconsciously fiddle with, for example, a loose-fitting ring. If you wear glasses and will be in a brightly lighted area, you should probably spray your glasses with an anti-glare spray (available in photography shops).

Women have more options in dress and more pitfalls. Very high heels can be tricky since they tend to throw a speaker off balance and make smooth, natural movement more difficult. Straight skirts are also risky, especially for the woman who will be seated on the platform before being introduced. A good idea is to sit in a chair and have someone check out just how much you will be revealing from the audience's perspective.

Clanking bracelets, hair styles that hide too much of the face, and shiny jewelry should be avoided. Beware of wearing a tight girdle. It makes breathing correctly difficult indeed. Taking along an extra pair of hose is a good insurance policy in case of a last-minute runner.

But men have their snares, too. Special attention should be given to the fit of the coat through the shoulders to be sure arms are free to move comfortably and without restriction. A precautionary measure for men is to empty your pockets before ascending the podium. Many a speech has been ruined by a speaker clanging his change or his keys in his pocket . . . usually without realizing he's doing it.

## POSTURE

Consider: A public speaker should appear "bigger than life." This has to do with bearing, taking space, stage presence, and an inner mind set.

The great Greek orator Demosthenes worked very hard to overcome his limitations as a speaker. One of his problems was his posture. To improve his bearing before an audience, he practiced speaking before a mirror with two swords hanging from the ceiling. The point of each sword barely touched his shoulders so that if he made any awkward movement, he would stab himself.[2] While this is not necessarily recommended as a re-hearsal technique, it does illustrate the importance a man with a centuries-long reputation as an outstanding speaker placed on posture.

Members of an audience will size you up from the moment they see you and decide—at least subconsciously—if you're go-ing to be worth hearing. Of course, the way you are dressed makes a statement, but another vital part of the message they receive about you is your posture and stage presence.

These are important points to keep in mind.

If you are seated on the platform before you speak, be aware that you are being watched and graded as a speaker be-fore you ever begin.

Lounging in your chair, or staring off into space gives a sloppy impression. Sitting up straight with an interested, in-volved-looking expression makes an initial good impression.

Also, beware of gripping the arms of your chair, wringing your hands, or making repetitive movements with your feet. These are tip-offs to nervousness and should be avoided.

Men should sit with both feet flat on the floor. Crossing one leg over the other usually results in doing strange things with your feet, such as moving one in a circular or swinging motion.

The safest thing for a woman is to sit with feet crossed at the ankle. This makes a more attractive line under the skirt and also helps keep your skirt down in front.

The way you get up from your chair is important also. Use your leg muscles to lift you quickly. More or less unfolding out of your chair looks sloppy and unenthusiastic.

Walk rapidly and with good posture and verve to the speaker's stand, making eye contact with the audience as you go. It's important to take space by showing outward confidence even before you utter the first word. The audience needs to know you are in command. Never start speaking before you get to the speaker's stand.

Once there say "thank you" to the person who introduced you. Pause and make eye contact with people in different sec-tions of the audience. Give your audience time to get used to seeing you there. Then begin your remarks.

During the speech, feet should be apart, approximately shoulder width. Weight should be equally distributed. Putting your weight on one foot throws your shoulders out of line and makes you as a speaker resemble the Leaning Tower of Pisa. It also leads to shifting your weight to the other foot and back and forth until you look like a rocking horse.

The head should be up so that the face, and especially the eyes, can be easily seen. If you are going to read a passage from a book (not a very long one, I hope), the book should be held up at chest level so that you can easily look up and continue to maintain eye contact.

Remember the lectern is there to hold your notes, not for use as a reclining couch. While resting your hands occasionally on the speaker's stand is acceptable, clutching it or leaning on it is strictly taboo.

Arms should be away from the body, not glued to your side like a tin soldier.

When using a microphone, be sure that it is adjusted to the proper level for your height. It should not cover your face or be positioned so that you cannot maintain solid, straight, and square posture. Don't fool with the mike stand or cord.

Beware of unconscious, distracting habits such as smoothing your hair, touching your nose, scratching, pulling on hair or clothing, playing with a pen or pencil. Ask a friend in the audience to note such behavior and report to you later.

Once you've finished, leave the speaker's stand with as much aplomb as you approached it. Shrugging your shoulders, showing disgust with yourself or acting as though you're glad that it's over can ruin an otherwise effective presentation.


## GESTURES

Consider: The fact that people respond 55 percent to your body language and expression, 37 percent to your vocal inflection and only 8 percent to what you say makes a rather startling statement about the importance of gestures.[3]

Hands? What to do with them?

One seasoned speaker says, "My biggest problem as a novice speaker was knowing what to do with those things hanging at the ends of my arms. All of a sudden it seemed as though they weighed at least fifty pounds each. No matter what I did with them, they seemed awkward and in the way. It took a bunch of speeches before I was able to turn my hands into assets instead of liabilities."

Few things about speaking can have a more positive or a more negative effect on the overall impact of the presentation than the use of gestures. Shakespeare, in *The Winter's Tale*, says: "There was speech in their dumbness, language in their very gesture."

There are three main benefits when gestures are used to advantage: gestures can be used to emphasize the main points of your presentation; good gestures allow your audience to better follow your presentation and your train of thought; and gestures may be used to involve your audience in what you're saying.

Let's start with some roles *not* to play with your hands as a speaker.

THE JEWELER—plays with ring, watch, etc.

THE PRAYER—folds hands in front of body, looks as though he's praying to just make it through.

THE STERN PARENT—stands with arms crossed over chest.

THE KEY EXECUTIVE—fiddles with keys, coins, and other wonderful things found in pockets.

THE FIG LEAF—stands with hands folded in front—much as Adam must have looked in his first outfit.

THE SOLDIER AT PARADE REST—holds hands behind back.

DISHPAN HANDS—conceals hands in pockets so no one can see them.

THE ATHLETIC TYPE—demonstrates athletic prowess with a running series of jabs, punches, uppercuts, karate chops, etc.[4]

Most speakers who play those roles get locked into position until it looks like rigor mortis has set in.

The antidote to being a rigid Robert or Ruth is to start with your arms held loosely by your sides, keeping space between your arms and your body. Don't hold them too close or you'll look stiff, as if your arms are glued down. With your arms by your side, they're ready to move freely, at your instant bidding.

Appropriate gestures can go a long way toward making your presentation more interesting and dramatic, keeping your

## HOW TO USE GESTURES

Gestures should be, or appear to be, spontaneous.

The whole body should be involved, not just a hand or a part of your arm.

They should be broad and sweeping with arms away from the body. Gestures with the upper arm held rigidly against the body look awkward, even grotesque. Move arms and hands from in front of your body out to the sides.

The larger the audience is, the broader the gestures must be in order to be effective.

Using the exact same gesture over and over gets dull and monotonous.

Avoid: self-touching movements, covering mouth, playing with mike, or pointer, gripping podium, wringing hands.

Your gestures and facial expressions should be a matching pair. For example, if you're talking about something frightening, have a fearful expression with your arm up as if protecting yourself.

Practice making very large, exaggerated gestures. Once you get used to really throwing those arms out there and around, you can bring them down to an appropriate size and they'll feel natural and comfortable.

Practice in front of a mirror or, better yet, with a video recorder to see how your movements look.

Be sure your body language isn't sending a message you don't want to say. For example, covering your mouth can tell your audience you're not sure of what you're saying or they may even get the impression that you're not telling the truth.

Remember that a speaker's stand forms a barrier between your audience and you. Stepping out from behind the stand can be very effective, especially when you want to seem more intimate in a certain part of your speech or when telling an anecdote that can be dramatized. If you can speak without notes, so much the better—don't use a lectern at all. If you are a frequent speaker, it might be worth your investment in your own lectern made of plastic or Lucite, allowing your audience to see all of you at all times. If you are unusually short, take along a platform to stand on. Otherwise, you will be dwarfed and appear child-like behind a huge speaker's stand.

audience's attention, and reinforcing what you're saying. But don't let gestures take precedence over your message. Remember, if the listener is paying more attention to what your arms and hands are doing than to what you're saying, you're being upstaged!

## EYE CONTACT

Consider: Eye contact forms a very personal bond with another person. It's an absolute essential for establishing good rapport with an audience.

Most people are very irritated by someone who will not look at them when they're carrying on a conversation. Looking down and glancing around gives the impression of untrustworthiness or less than honesty. Staring off in space says, "I'm bored" or "I'm not interested." We want to talk with someone who will look at us—both when we're talking and when they're talking. The same is true of talking with someone in an audience.

The eye—probably more than any other part of the body—gives us a glimpse into the mind of the other person. It's interesting to note that it can give us definite cues as to how what we're saying is being received. If the pupil enlarges, it tells us that the person is reacting positively to what we are saying.

There are several benefits to maintaining eye contact with your audience.

1.  You give the impression that you are truly interested in the listeners when you look them in the eye and maintain that contact for several seconds. The major benefit of this eye contact is that you can establish rapport quickly and easily.

2.  Looking at someone without hesitancy projects confidence, power, and authority. It also conveys openness and honesty.

3.  Eye contact involves the audience and helps keep them interested in what you're saying.

Here are some points to remember about eye contact.

Eye contact with your audience should begin the moment you are introduced as a speaker—as you rise and walk to the speaker's stand.

After saying "thank you" to the person who introduced you, you should pause and make eye contact with people in several sections of your audience. The audience needs that time to look at you and get ready to listen. It also shows confidence and helps you to "take charge."

Eye contact in the beginning of your remarks is extremely important as you make that vital first impression as a speaker. Your opening remarks should be committed to memory so that you are free to look at the audience without distraction.

In order to establish solid eye contact, look at a person from three to five seconds. This gives the listeners the impression you are speaking just to them and makes your remarks seem personal.

Glancing at a person for only a second and then changing to someone else gives a shifty look and lessens confidence in what you have to say. An excellent example of the adverse effect of darting eye glances is the Nixon-Kennedy debate during their campaign for president. It is interesting to note that the majority of listeners who heard the debate on radio credited Nixon with winning. However, those who watched the debates on television gave Kennedy the victory. Analysts attributed Nixon's frequently shifting eye movements to the viewers' reaction of less confidence in what he said.

Looking at one person for more than about five seconds makes the person feel as though he or she is being stared at and results in discomfort for that individual.

Avoiding eye contact with your audience sends a message of guilt or dishonesty or that you're not leveling with the listeners.

Be careful whom you look at if what you're saying is "preachy" or can be considered a reprimand. The person may conclude that your remarks are directed at him or her personally, and that you are using a public occasion to embarrass or get even.

Establish eye contact with a person in one area of your audience, then move to another section and so on. Concentrating on one part of the audience for too long a time results in people in other areas of the room feeling left out.

Conversely, looking at a person with a "show me" look with arms folded, or looking at a watch, can be disconcerting. For

# HOW TO USE FACIAL EXPRESSIONS

There are several benefits to using good facial expressions.

1. Facial expressions help you to set the mood for your audience. When you smile or laugh, it cues them to get ready for something light or less serious. With a somber expression, you help them prepare for something of a more serious nature.

2. Your expressions convey that you are human, that you have a personality, and that you are a regular person—just like your listeners.

3. Good facial expressions help your audience to follow your line of thought and alert them to what their reaction should be.

Here are some helpful hints on making facial expressions a real asset in speaking.

Maintain an overall pleasant countenance—even if you're talking about a very serious subject. Speakers who frown and grimace the whole time make members of the audience feel as though they've been hit with a bat.

Make sure what you're saying with your face matches what you're saying with your tongue. If the two don't agree, the result can be confusing to your audience. But it also can be skillfully used to produce laughter since incongruity is one form of humor.

Use your facial expressions with reinforcing gestures to get and keep you audience's attention.

Learn to be an actor—especially when telling anecdotes and using other illustrative material.

Practice in front of a mirror or with video equipment.

Your facial expressions should appear natural and spontaneous, not forced or contrived.

You can convey friendliness and a genuine interest in your audience with the look on your face.

In speaking, your face truly can be your fortune . . . if it's used to best advantage.

your own mental health, try to look at friendly faces.

Being tied to your notes or script prohibits your making and maintaining good eye contact and results in less interest in your presentation. When reading from a book, hold the book up at chest level, so that you can glance up every few seconds and look at your audience. Limit the length of the passage to be read. Paraphrase part of it.

The fine art of eye contact is a vital skill that must be developed in order to be a successful speaker. It can go a long way toward making you appear to be confident, personable, competent, friendly, honest, and in control.

## FACIAL EXPRESSIONS

Consider: The expression on your face reinforces what you are saying (or certainly should), adds subtle facets to your meaning, and can go a long way toward keeping the attention of your audience. An animated facial expression is a potent tool for involving your audience with you as a speaker.

Most people do not like to carry on really important conversations over the telephone. Do you know why? We want to see the other person's reaction to our words. And we want to be sure we're understanding his or her meaning. That means we have to be looking at the other person as well as hearing the words that are being spoken. Just the voice alone doesn't tell the whole story.

Research has shown that a very high percentage of learning takes place through the sense of sight. Remember, the average person learns 87 percent by sight. Hearing is next highest with only 7 percent. As speakers, those figures should have a tremendous impact on what we do. Obviously we have to give our listeners something to see as well as to hear. And they have to go together.

The expressionless speaker who stands in one position throughout a speech is inviting the audience's minds to wander to other things. If you don't give them something interesting to watch, they're going to be painting more interesting mental pictures in their mind's eye. Since the human face, supposedly, is capable of 250,000 different expressions, there should be no reason for a speaker to stand with a deadpan expression.

# 3

# *The Mechanics of Speaking*

## YOU ARE WHAT YOU EAT

Consider: As a speaker, you are what you eat.

Want to really program yourself for failure as a speaker? Then eat a huge meal right before you speak, or have a cocktail or two—just to loosen up.

It's tough to be an after-dinner speaker and just sit and pick at your food—especially if it looks and smells delicious. But it's definitely the prudent thing to do.

When you eat a lot, your blood vessels shunt your blood supply away from other parts of your body to your digestive organs. Since that includes your brain, the result is a drop in mental sharpness and response. You experience post-prandial drowsiness which is in direct ratio to how much you "pigged out." You also have, as a result, less physical energy—something every speaker needs in super abundance.

As a speaker, you also need to be aware that the same thing is happening to your audience if they've just eaten a big meal. As a speaker, you may have to use your ingenuity to keep them awake.

One speaker said: "In my travels abroad, I am frequently struck by the fact that most civilized nations allow for a sensible siesta after the noonday meal. The United States stands almost alone in its insistence upon a more rigorous approach. I refer, of course, to our quaint custom of forcing those who have just eaten heartily to digest a full-fledged speech along with their meat and potatoes."[1]

Some other cautions: chocolate is particularly bad for the voice and carbonated drinks can be hazardous to your speaking, especially if you have a tendency to burp. Nervousness will often result in a dry mouth and a tense throat, but the answer is not to drink ice water. That will only make the throat tighter. Taking a few sips of a warm drink is better. Or if that's not available, lightly bring your teeth down several times on your tongue. In a few seconds, there will be enough saliva to overcome a dry mouth.

Never ... don't ever ... whatever you do ... don't drink any alcoholic beverages before you speak. There's one chance in a thousand that you'll come across as urbane and witty as you think you are if you do.


## VOICE

Consider: Your voice is the instrument that you must use to convey your message. It has an infinite variety of pitch, level, and tones. You need to learn to play on it just as an accomplished musician coaxes inspired and beautiful sounds from a violin.

Perhaps you have noticed how often we form opinions of others by the sound of their voices. We say, "I have never met him, but he sounds nice over the telephone."

Each person has been given a certain type of voice which is one of the things that makes you unique as an individual. All of us can learn to use our voices more effectively with training and concentrated effort. Few of us ever really develop the full potential of our vocal mechanisms to sway and influence others in speaking.

A must for improving your speaking voice and speech is a tape recorder. None of us sounds the way we think we do. If you're not accustomed to hearing your own voice as others hear it, it will be a real shocker at first. Listen and ask yourself this question, "Do I have the kind of voice, the enthusiasm and clarity in speaking that I would find easy to listen to myself?" If your answer is "no" or "not quite," now's the time to do something about it.

Remember what Fred Glanz, world champion hog caller,

said: "You've got to have appeal as well as power in your voice. You've got to convince the hogs you've got something for them."

## Vocal Energy

Probably one of the most important things a speaker can do to keep the audience's attention is to maintain a high level of vocal energy throughout the presentation. Vocal energy projects enthusiasm and excitement on the part of the speaker. If you don't appear to be enthusiastic and excited about what you're saying, why would anyone want to listen?

Mac Douglass said: "Burning desire will reflect itself in fiery words. Excitement and enthusiasm are essential to successful speaking and go hand in hand with a presenter's level of confidence."[2] It also has to do with the speaker's vocal energy. Regardless of how enthusiastic you may feel about your subject, unless you project that enthusiasm through a high level of energy vocally, your audience will never know.

## Vocal Pitch

Do you sound as good as you look? After listening to yourself on the tape recorder, decide if you have any of these voice flaws.

| | |
|---|---|
| Breathy | Adolescent |
| Whiny | Nasal twang |
| Whispery | Screechy |
| High-pitched | Strident |
| Chirpy | Shrill |

Or do you have a firm, strong, low-pitched, colorful voice? A low-pitched voice is soft, soothing, persuasive. It also shows power and commands attention. Would you believe that Lauren Bacall once had a high-pitched voice? Not only high, but high and nasal, according to the late Howard Hawks, the film director credited with giving her her start in films.

When Hawks first met Bacall the first thing he noticed was a little tiny, nasal voice as she asked for work. "I had to be honest," he recalled. "I said that the lines we had, the stories, were not made for a high nasal voice." She left and, to his amazement, returned in about three weeks. When she said "Hello," she sounded like a different person. "I had to admire her," he remembered. "She wanted to work and she had to have put forth much time and effort to accomplish this."[3]

What if you—like Lauren Bacall—have a naturally high-pitched, irritating-sounding voice? You can do something about it.

The point is not to try to force it lower but to coax it lower by relaxing your throat muscles. Tense throat muscles can create an artificially high voice. First of all, train your own ears to locate the proper pitch for your voice. Put your hand on your chest and lower your voice a half tone at a time on the phrase "I think it is not going to snow" until it gets uncomfortable. At that point, sensibly go back up one tone.

A good way to keep reminding yourself to stay at this lower level is to find the note on a piano keyboard and then, from time to time, read aloud by the piano—hitting the note again and again and matching your pitch to it.

To gently stretch and deepen your voice, say "King Kong, ding dong, bing bong." Each time go lower in tone so that your last "bong" is easing down into that strange gravelly range. Never force this sound! Just let it ease out. Bit by bit, your voice will be led down in tone and some of the high-pitched tightness will leave your voice.

One cause of a higher-pitched voice is nervousness which results in tensing the vocal cords and throat muscles. Happily there are exercises to relax your throat. Do them a couple of times a day until you can prove to your own satisfaction that you have lowered your pitch.

1. Sitting, let your head hang forward as though you had no neck supporting it. Shut your eyes for five very slow counts.

2. Lie on your back on the floor, knees bent. Concentrate on each part of your body—from feet to head—in sequence, willing it to relax. Breathe in to the slow count of six, then gradually exhale to the slow count of six before going to the next part of your body.

3. Now sit up and, with your head rolling slowly in a circle—first clockwise and then counter clockwise—say "I am relaxed . . . I am completely relaxed."

Say it over and over again, starting with scarcely more than a whisper. Then, very gradually, increase your volume until you're speaking at a normal volume. You'll notice a lower pitch to your voice.

But what if your voice is nasal? The main cause of nasality is a tight jaw or tension in the muscles in the back of the tongue. If you don't open your mouth when you speak, the sound has to come through your nose.

These exercises will help overcome an unpleasant twang.

1. Yawn elaborately, extravagantly, exaggeratedly. But remember to breathe normally and keep your shoulders and neck uninvolved.
2. Open your mouth only slightly, keeping your lower jaw as relaxed as possible. Then make an ah sound while moving your lower jaw rapidly from side to side.
3. To get accustomed to hearing your sound come out of your mouth instead of your nose, hold one palm in front of your lips and blow into it while saying "Whisssh." Say it over and over again. Your breath should be coming out in tiny explosions.

## Vocal Range

Most people do not begin to take advantage of the full vocal range of their speaking voice.

Speaking in a monotone voice—on basically the same note—can be an opiate to the listener and deadly dull even if the nodders manage to keep their eyes open. Your listeners may think of you and wish to hear you next time they have insomnia, but chances are they won't want to hear you again as a speaker. A monotone speaker has little chance of getting the message across. He's just too hard to listen to.

Even if you aren't a Johnny one-note speaker, you can improve your vocal range and effectiveness as a speaker by concentrated effort.

Try selecting a passage to read. Find your most comfortable pitch on the piano, then read the passage at a lower note and a higher note. Go about three notes higher and three or four notes lower than your starting pitch. Then read the passage using the full range.

You might even want to try singing the passage (even if it's in the shower) to really see how variety of pitch can enhance color and meaning of your words.

You'll find you'll gain variety ... and the interest of your audience.

### Vocal Level

People who fail to speak loudly enough communicate doubt and indecision to the listener. It also gives the impression that they are tired, lack energy, are unenthusiastic, or are in poor health.

Here are a couple of clues.

Do others often ask you to repeat yourself?

Do they appear to be straining to hear you, possibly by leaning their heads a bit closer or turning an ear toward you?

Speaking up is vital to the public speaker ... to executive advancement. According to Edward J. Hegarty, a nationally known lecturer, "The voice that is difficult to hear doesn't show confidence, indicate enthusiasm or demonstrate leadership qualities."[4]

Here are some suggestions to ensure your listeners will actually hear what you say.

Hold your head up. It's not likely that the listener will hear you if you're talking to your chest. Seeing the formation of your words also helps the other person understand what you are saying—especially if there is any kind of hearing problem.

Project your voice. Throw it out audience, just as you would a baseball. A good projection tip is to imagine your words coming from the diaphragm, exiting without friction through your throat and chest, to be placed on an imaginary shelf 3 to 4 feet in front of you.

Open your mouth wider. Closed-mouth talkers are difficult to understand. Practice talking with a wide-open mouth. It will add volume to your voice.

Assume the listener is slightly deaf and you'll have to speak a little louder to be heard. It is better to be slightly too loud than not loud enough to be heard.

Be aware of noises you may have to overcome, such as air conditioning or a speaker in the meeting room next door.

A few cautions about vocal level and the use of a microphone.

Don't substitute a mike for good speaking technique. You still need to project your voice.

Be sure to speak into the mike and have it properly positioned, depending on the type of microphone you're using.

If you are a speaker who tends to get very loud in places, back a little away from the mike. You don't want to deafen the audience.

Be sure the microphone level is appropriately set for you as a speaker. You should check it out before the meeting begins. It is also a good idea to have someone monitor the level while you are speaking since a room full of people alters the way sound carries. While you want the level high enough, be sure it is not set so loud that you are actually hurting your listener's ears.

Don't forget to vary your volume level, making sure it's still being heard. Lowering your voice can produce a very intimate, confidential moment between the speaker and the audience. Getting louder can produce a dramatic build toward a climax. You might want to consider using a stage whisper for an especially dramatic statement.

## Delivery Rate

Just as you need variety in pitch and speaking level, you also need to vary your speed in speaking.

As a whole, you will want to speak a little bit faster than your normal conversational rate when speaking before an audience for several reasons.

1. Your listener will be thinking at a rate four times faster than most people speak. A little more rapid pace will help compensate for this difference.
2. A more rapid pace projects enthusiasm and energy.
3. People are convinced that people who speak faster are brighter.
4. Recent experiments conducted by James MacLachlan showed that speaking somewhat faster than usual: enhanced the speaker's persuasiveness; increased the speaker's ratings on trust and knowledge; improved information recall among listeners. Overall, a 25 percent increase in the speaker's delivery rate was preferred by a substantial majority of those tested.[5]

Here are some other important things to keep in mind about the pace you use in speaking.

If you are speaking away from your area of the country, keep in mind the speaking rate of your listeners. You should speak a little faster than they do—but not too much faster. For example, Southerners, accustomed to a slower rate of speech in everyday life, will have trouble adjusting to an extremely rapid-fire speaker. The opposite is also true. An Eastern audience will go to sleep listening to a speaker from the South—especially one with a marked Southern accent—unless the speaker makes a marked effort to speed up.

Speaking at the same rate all the time gets monotonous. Speed up. Slow down, especially when you want to emphasize a certain point.

Don't be afraid to stop talking. Silence is the punctuation of speech, just as a semicolon, a period, or a new paragraph is to written communication. A dramatic pause can be more powerful at times than any words you might say. If you ask the audience a question, be still so that they really have time to reflect on it and mentally answer your question.

Unless you have excellent diction, you cannot speak rapidly and be easily understood.

## BREATH CONTROL

Consider: Using your voice without adequate breath support is like an elephant trying to walk on bird legs.

Have you ever had your voice go completely out of control when you're nervous? Most people have at one time or another. What happens is that stage fright results in a souped up respiratory rate. And the more shallowly we breathe, the less support we have for our voices.

There are three types of breathing.

**Clavicular breathing** is from the top portions of the chest. It is the least desirable method for speakers because they cannot get sufficient air to last them while they deliver a complete thought. It also does not provide the necessary support system to produce a well-modulated, controlled sound. This type of breathing usually tips the audience off that the speaker is nervous.

**Thoracic breathing** is normal chest breathing. Air quantity is sufficient for conversation and usual physical activity.

**Abdominal or diaphragmatic breathing** is the preferred type for public speaking because the air quantity is maximized. In abdominal breathing, the abdominal muscles are used to help expand the chest fully. Athletes use diaphragmatic breathing. They have to in order to run the race.

Have you ever watched a baby breathe? Babies breathe from the diaphragm naturally. As we get older, most of us switch to thoracic breathing unless we have a need to breathe more deeply.

To practice breathing from the diaphragm, place your hand between the two halves of your rib cage and inhale. If you are breathing deeply enough, you should feel your diaphragm expand like a balloon. Exhale and you will feel it go down.

Another good way to check is to lie down on your back and place a lightweight book on your stomach. It should go up and down as you breathe.

If you are not accustomed to abdominal breathing, build up to it gradually. Breathing deeply too much to begin with can result in dizziness.

There are several major benefits to be gained from breathing from the diaphragm.

1.  First, it has a calming effect on you; the opposite is true of shallow breathing.
2.  It gives you control over your voice. It helps your voice mind you.
3.  It provides the support your voice needs. This is especially important for those who speak, sing, or otherwise use their voices extensively
4.  It results in a richer, fuller, more resonant tone. The contraction of the diaphragm enlarges the chest cavity. The larger chamber enables you to produce a fuller, rounder speaking voice that carries and projects better.
5.  Speaking from the diaphragm allows you to speak with greater intensity and provides greater range for dramatic emphasis. Try it for yourself. Say "What do you mean?" as you normally would and then say the same sentence from the diaphragm.

There are several things you can do to develop the habit of breathing from the diaphragm and to control the flow of your breath in speaking.

Here are some suggestions.

Inhale on the count of five, hold your breath for a count of five, then exhale saying "ea-sy" slowly.

Inhale. Exhale evenly on a count of ten.

Tighten the diaphragm muscles above your waist as if someone was about to punch you and you wanted to block the blow. Release. Breathe fairly deeply so your ribs expand to the sides and back, then tighten those diaphragm muscles and exhale slowly with control to a count of ten, twenty, thirty, forty—whatever you can comfortably handle. Make a "ssss" sound through your teeth as you do it, if no one is listening. Otherwise, do it silently. This is also a good relaxation exercise when you are tense.

## DICTION

Consider: We read in the Bible (I Cor. 9:14) "Except ye utter by the tongue words easy to be understood, how shall it be known what is spoken? For ye shall speak into the air."

What you say is important, but the way you say your words is critical—if you are to be understood. Unfortunately, most Americans are lip lazy in comparison with many people from other countries. Have you ever really watched a Frenchman speak? He makes all kinds of faces and uses his lips energetically, non-stop. He has to in order to make the sounds in his language correctly.

We need to take a cue from the Frenchman in that regard in order to produce the sounds of the English language correctly ... and so that they can be easily understood. Mumblers chew their words and don't use the facial muscles necessary for clear enunciation.

Here are some suggestions to improve the clarity of your speech.

First, practice reading aloud with a tape recorder and actually hear where you need to improve. Increase your speed, reading as rapidly as you possibly can and still form your sounds correctly and understandably.

Open your mouth when you speak.

Move your lips.

Practice putting on the final consonant sounds. This is probably the most common mistake in enunciation. Often a speaker will end up saying something entirely different from what is meant. For example, if the speaker says, "Sometimes a little help is all a person needs . . ." but fails to put the "p" on the word "help," the listener will definitely get a different message from the one intended.

Also watch beginning consonants. Some speakers have a habit of dropping occasional initial beginnings, which can also be dangerous.

Also be sure you are forming vowel sounds properly. These are some good words to practice in this regard.

mate mote mute moot

rack reck rock ruck rook

bah boil beau boo

There are a number of often used, simple words which are commonly mispronounced. Practice saying these words correctly:

ar-c-tic

Feb-ru-ary

r-oo-f

congr-at-ulate

fi-f-th

stren-g-th

cr-ee-k

Gover-n-ment

w-h-at

d-a-is

man-u-facture

e-du-cation

per-h-aps

lib-ra-ry

Pay particular attention to words ending in "ing." All too often "going" comes out "gonna," "running" sounds like "runnen."

Also, take care in saying the word "you." Far too many speakers say "don't cha" instead of "don't you."

Then there are the charlatan words that masquerade as

words but really aren't words at all. Some of the most common are:

irregardless for regardless
wisht for wish
accidently for accidentally
anywheres for anywhere
furtherest for furthest
hunderd for hundred
unawares for unaware
heighth for height
undoubtably for undoubtedly

A good exercise to improve enunciation and projection is the whisper drill. While whispering, exaggerate the functions of the mouth, lips, and tongue. To be heard across the room, the speaker will be forced to make a clean break of all the words and to slow this whispered speech to the point that the vocal muscles can manage each word distinctly.

Listen to good speakers—on the platform, on television, on radio. Notice how meticulously they speak . . . correctly and yet not pedantically.

As you begin to clean up and polish your diction, your speech will seem stilted, perhaps ostentatious. But before long, you will find yourself speaking correctly as a matter of course.

Be on the lookout for slovenly speech. Snap off the ends of your words. Put crispness into your words. Show purpose in each word you utter. Most of all, don't let your method of speaking sabotage the message of your speech.

Remember Shakespeare's admonition to "Speak the speech I pray you . . . trippingly on the tongue."

## SILENCE—THE PAUSE THAT REFRESHES

Consider: "Talking is like playing the harp. There is as much in laying the hands on the strings to stop their vibration as in twanging them to bring out their music."—Oliver Wendell Holmes[6]

Unfortunately too many would-be orators think it is absolutely necessary to hear the sound of their voices at all times—without pause or relief to the audience. As a result, they keep talking—even when they don't have words to say. This results in a steady stream of non-words or meaningless fillers which in over-abundance can be very distracting—even extremely annoying to the listener.

The sad thing about it is that using padding or filler sounds can become such an ingrained habit that the speaker is not even aware it's a problem. But the audience will be very much aware that it is a problem. In fact, when carried to extremes, the audience may even tune out the message because of the mess of meaningless sounds.

Probably the worst culprit is "uh" or "er." Frances Rodman tells us that "Many after-dinner speakers remind us that to 'er-r' is human."[7], Dorothy Sarnoff whimsically quotes Genesis 38:7: "Er was wicked in the sight of the Lord; and the Lord slew him." She maintains that "the Lord was right. To err is human, but to 'er' should be considered a capital crime. My only complaint about the slaying of Er is that it should have been done before he had a chance to start a family; his descendants today threaten to take over the world."[8]

There's no doubt about it. "Er" does have a whole family with criminal tendencies. How many times have you suffered through a tirade of: "uh," "like," "y'know," "see what I mean," "o.k.?," "well," "man," "right?"

Not as bad, but not good either, is an endless stream of unnecessary connector words like "and," "so," "well," "now," and "o.k." that can turn several paragraphs into one long, out-of-control sentence. Perhaps you've had the experience of listening to speakers who never end a sentence. It can become a game, almost, wondering when they're going to have to pause long enough to come up for air.

The same word or phrase that is used repetitively can become filler material also and almost as distracting. Think about your pet phrases and start noticing if you use them excessively in conversation. If so, you, no doubt, will do the same thing before an audience.

The remedy for these common maladies—short of gagging the speaker—is silence, the pause that refreshes. There are several benefits of using a pause in speaking.

1.  Filler sounds distract your audience. Pausing periodically will call your audience's attention more

forcefully to the words you say.

2. Silence is the punctuation of speech. It lets the audience know when you've come to the end of a thought, when you're ready to make a transition.

3. A carefully placed pause will allow you to drive your points home, and gives the audience time to absorb your points and reflect on what you've said.

4. The pause gives you, as a speaker, an opportunity to collect your thoughts and to move around if you start feeling tense.

5. A moment of silence also gives you time to catch your breath and enables you to use your voice more effectively.

Sandy Livner, president of a public speaking firm, believes that pauses are very important tools in speaking effectively. She says, "A person who knows how to pause at the right time—who controls a period of silence—comes across as being more authoritative than the person who doesn't."[9]

George Jessel said that he learned his best trick from George M. Cohan who "taught me how to pause while talking to an audience so as to make them believe that I was thinking of something important, or some new line that had just come to mind—when it was actually something tried and true that I knew would get a laugh."[10]

These are some good things to remember about eliminating filler sounds and meaningless words and the effective use of the pause.

Chances are if you use padding as a public speaker, you also use it in conversation. Since awareness is the first step toward correcting the habit, get your spouse or a close friend to help you become conscious of the extent of your habit. Get someone you're around a lot to give you a silent signal, e.g., pulling the ear, touching the nose, each time you use a speech filler.

Check yourself out with a tape recorder. Tell a story and play it back. You may be surprised how many times you say "uh" and "you know." Even better, next time you speak in public have someone record your remarks and check them out when you get home.

Silence can be used to give your presentation more impact

and to add interest. A dramatic pause can be a potent tool for a speaker. Use the pause to give emphasis to a certain word or phrase in a sentence. Silence can help build suspense, especially in telling a story.

Silence can be used as an attention-getting device. If several people are looking around, stop talking. You'll get their attention. It also can be used to stop a distracting activity of audience members. For example, if two people are talking, stop and look at them. As a rule, it won't be long before they'll grow uncomfortable and get silent themselves.

Be sure to pause briefly after each sentence and longer after each paragraph. There are some cautions, however, in using the pause: Don't pause so much that it seems there are gaps in your speech pattern and don't pause so long that it seems like you've forgotten your speech.

## DIFFERENCES IN ORAL AND WRITTEN LANGUAGE

Consider: Oral and written languages are quite different in several ways. Even though you may be an excellent writer, you will not be an excellent speaker if you use the same approach in speaking that you do for the written word.

Written language must be ultimately intelligible to the reader. Spoken language must be instantly intelligible to the listener. You only have one chance.

Spoken language is less formal. The style used in public speaking should lie somewhere between the written word and conversation.

Spoken language is more repetitive. It is important to rephrase several times key ideas you want the listeners to take away with them.

Spoken language is more idiomatic. Otherwise, it sounds somewhat stilted and stuffy.

Spoken language should be simpler in structure than written language. The subject, verb, and object must stand out and not be overwhelmed with a lot of parenthetical clauses. Otherwise, the listener will have a hard time following your train of thought.

Spoken language is more likely to include questions.

The length of sentences in spoken language is less uniform. Short sentences are shorter. Long sentences are longer.

Figurative language adds life and color to spoken words. Imaginative metaphors, similes, and alliteration can turn an otherwise pedestrian speech into a memorable one.

Examples:

Lincoln described a nation "conceived in liberty."

Kennedy spoke of freedom as a "torch passed to a new generation."[11]

J.F. Bere, chairman of Borg-Wagner Corporation, described untapped human assets as "waiting like a coiled spring to release enormous potentials ..." Problems were discussed as "smoldering fires" and new programs as being structured "a brick here, a brick there."[12]

There's also a difference in rhythm. Take a cue from the musician who uses rhythm and cadence to intrigue listeners and to move the music to a climax. The speaker can also involve listeners and stir them by the sheer force of the rhythm and cadence of the language to heights of grandeur. The repetition of a word, a phrase, or a statement has an effect like that of a repeated theme in music which is used with variations. A good example comes from a speech given by U.S. Circuit Judge Abner J. Mikva: "These are trying times for all of us, yet I believe that trying times are a time to try. Not a time to shrug a shoulder in disgust and turn your back on the problems. Not a time to say that things are in a mess and will probably just get worse. And most definitely not a time to conclude that there is nothing a single individual can do."[13] And, of course, one of the classics is Martin Luther King's "I Have a Dream" speech. He used the phrase "I have a dream..." seven times, preceding phrases such as: "... every valley shall be exalted," "... every hill and mountain shall be made low," "... the rough places will be made plane," "... the glory of the Lord shall be revealed." He also used "Let freedom ring..." ten times.[14]

Oral language uses more contractions.

Since a written speech must be read, it is important to read it aloud to check on flow of words and phrases and for spots which may be difficult to get your tongue around.

# 4

# *Involving Your Audience*

## FINDING YOUR COMMON GROUND WITH AN AUDIENCE

Consider: You can be the most polished speaker in the world and still fall flat on your face if you leave out one of the most important ingredients of a successful speech—finding out everything possible about your audience and tailoring your content, techniques, and involvement approaches to their needs and intellectual level.

Someone has wisely said: "An effective speech starts where the audience is and ends where the speaker wants them to be." Not finding out, in advance, where the audience is guarantees a less than effective speech.

If you've ever tried to use exactly the same speech with two very different types of audience, you have probably learned the wisdom of adapting your remarks to the level and interests of each individual group. Of course, that's a part of the challenge and excitement of public speaking—learning how to move a particular audience to your point of view.

It's important to find your common ground with your audience. Every speech begins with the speaker . . .

here . . . and the audience . . . over there.

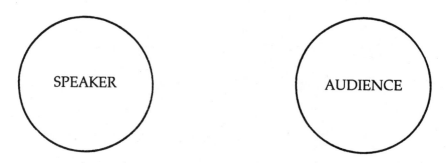

In order to communicate effectively, you have to move closer together. The secret is to find some things you have in common with your audience . . . to move to "common ground."

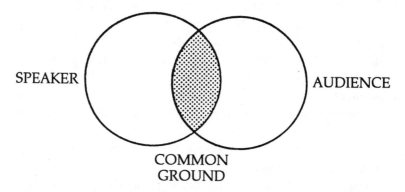

There are four main areas where you can find common ground with your listeners: common needs, shared interests, mutual concerns, and same experiences.

## DOING AN AUDIENCE ANALYSIS

Consider: Each speech, in order to be effective, must be tailor-made for that particular audience.

Remember what Aristotle said: "Of the three elements in speech making—speaker, subject and persons addressed—it is the last one, the hearer, that determines the speech's end and object."

Your first step in ensuring a successful experience—both for you and your audience—is to find out as much as possible about the people who will be listening to you and as much as possible about that particular occasion.

For several reasons you need to know how many people will be there. The style of presentation will vary with the audience's size. In general, the larger the audience is, the more formal the presentation. The size of the audience determines the effectiveness of various audio-visual approaches.

Audience participation techniques vary with the number of people. As a rule of thumb, the larger the audience is, the more difficult it is to get participation. Audience size will also determine whether or not you may want to use handout materials and what type of materials.

You will need to find out all you can about the makeup of the audience. What will be the average age? Talking about events that occurred long before most of your listeners were born makes it difficult for them to relate to your examples . . . and to you.

What will be the ethnic makeup of the audience? Will several races be represented or basically only one? If you are speaking to a group of a different racial background than your own, it's a good idea to get someone you know from that background to check out the material you plan to use and to offer suggestions for relating to that particular group.

What is the average educational background and level of sophistication of your audience? This should be kept in mind in your choice of terms, vocabulary, and also anecdotes, quotes, etc. Charts, tables, and graphs impress highly technical, well-educated audiences. With a lower level group, the more authoritarian the speaker, the better he or she will be accepted.

What will be the percentage of men and the percentage of women in the audience? As a general rule, men are more receptive to facts; women, to people-related information.

What are the occupations of the listeners? This will be especially helpful in selecting anecdotal material which they can relate to. It also will assist you in knowing whether to take a mainly factual, logical approach or a more inspirational, idea- and emotion-sparking tack. People in professions such as engineering and accounting would, for the most part, respond more positively to the former, while those in social services or the arts would usually be better reached by the latter approach.

What are their special interests, affiliations, and religious backgrounds?

A good technique is to profile an average member of your audience by asking yourself these questions.

Who is he?

Why is she listening to me?

What does he want or need?

What does she like?

What does he already know?

What does she believe?

What is his self-image?

What is her image of me?

What are his interests?

What is her language, including slang and jargon?

What motivates him?

How much will she be interested in knowing about my subject?

Why were you asked to speak to this particular audience about this particular topic (if you were given a special subject)? How much does the audience already know about your subject? You don't want to insult their intelligence if they're already rather knowledgeable on the subject, but neither do you want to be speaking over their heads. How much do they need to know or want to know?

What are the attitudes of the audience toward this subject? Do they have any specific interests in relation to this topic?

What does the audience know about you? What is their general attitude toward you and the organization you represent?

Do they have any strongly held beliefs and attitudes you either would want to address or avoid?

Are there any especially sensitive topics or any recent local events that might relate to the subject of your speech? For example, if you are a school superintendent speaking on employee relations to a group of school administrators whose teachers are out on strike, it would definitely make a difference in what you would say.

Will a question-and-answer session be appropriate? If so,

try to anticipate the types of questions this particular group will ask. Find out if the program chairman has heard comments from members of the group that would relate to your subject.

There are several other things about the meeting arrangements that you need to check out with the program chairman or the person who invited you to speak. How long should your presentation be? If a question-and-answer session is to be held, will additional time be provided in the program? It is very important to stay within the time limit given, and very rude to go over the allotted time. How will the meeting room be arranged? Will a meal be served before you speak? Will your presentation be the only one or will there be other speakers? Is audio-visual equipment available if you wish to use it? Can it be used effectively in that particular setting?

You also need to find out about the particular group or organization you've been invited to address and if this is a special occasion of some type.

When speaking away from home, avoid colloquialisms that may not be understood. Be aware that expressions common to your part of the country can have a different meaning to an audience in another area. This is particularly true if you are speaking in another country. A case in point is the Londoner who was asked to say a few words at a luncheon in Taipei. Since he did not speak Chinese, his remarks were translated by an interpreter. His words, "I just want you to know that I'm tickled to death to be here," came out in translation as, "This poor man scratches himself until he dies, only to be with you."

All of the previously discussed approaches to analyzing your audience should be done before the speaking engagement. However, audience analysis should not end there. It should continue as you arrive at the event, before it begins, while others are eating, speaking, or what have you, and even during your speech.

Plan to arrive a little early to check out the "lay of the land." This is especially important if you are speaking in an unfamiliar setting or to a group you do not know. Talk to as many people as you possibly can before the meeting begins. This will give you a good feel for your audience and will help build rapport. It also helps to see a few friendly faces staring back at you instead of a roomful of strangers. An excellent rapport builder is to

mention what a member of the group (by name) said to you a-
bout the subject before the meeting.

Be very observant of what takes place in the meeting before
you speak. If there are other speakers before you, take advantage of their turn at the lectern to find out the audience's reaction to various speaking approaches. For example, if they are
not very responsive in reacting to humor, you might want to
leave out any jokes that will really fall flat if no one laughs . . . or
even snickers.

While you are speaking, watch your listeners like a hawk.
Are they giving you clues that they're uncomfortable by fan-
ning, putting on jackets, rubbing their arms, etc.? If so, have the
room temperature adjusted.

Are you keeping their attention? If they're looking at their
watches (or even worse, holding them up to their ear to see if
they're still running), fidgeting, nodding, or whatever, you need
to do something, and quick. Here are some signs of inattention
and some possible remedies.

*Signal:* Nodding heads.

*Solution:* Lower room temperature; increase your volume;
have the audience raise their hands, stand, or say a word or
phrase to a neighbor; move out into the audience.

*Signal:* Members of audience whispering.

*Solution:* Get quiet; look directly at talkers; ask one of them
a question.

*Signal:* Puzzled looks on faces.

*Solution:* Restate your point in simpler language; give an
illustration; show how it relates to something in the listeners'
experience; use a diagram or a drawing if a chalkboard, a flip
chart, or an overhead transparency is readily available.

*Signal:* Questions being asked that have already been answered, or irrelevant remarks.

*Solution:* Take a different approach in restating your position; in case of a persistent questioner or an argumentative
person, offer to discuss the question afterwards.

*Signal:* People looking at watches or at clock at back of
room.

*Solution:* Summarize the remainder of your talk, take a
break, or do something totally unexpected.

Be alert to body language. What are they saying back to

you as you speak? These are some generally accepted messages listeners give a speaker by what they do.

> Folding arms across chest—closed mind or hostile response
> Moving chair forward, leaning forward toward speaker—open-mindedness, interest in message
> Crossing legs—competitive attitude, opposition
> Stroking chin—undecided, contemplating
> Stroking cheek—receptive
> Open hands—willingness to listen
> Hands behind head—taking it all in
> Fidgeting, looking around—bored
> Swinging foot in circle, tapping foot—bored, impatient
> Wrinkled brow—puzzled, contemplating
> Wringing hands—nervous, anxious
> Twiddling thumbs—bored
> Shrugging shoulders—indifference
> Gritting teeth—anger
> Rolling eyes—disgust
> Dropping mouth open—disbelief
> Covering mouth with hand—surprise, shock
> Biting lip—concentration, thinking
> Looking off in distance—indifference, daydreaming
> Touching nose with index finger quickly—doubt
> Glancing sideways, drawing back—suspicion
> Steepling hands—confidence

Become an eye watcher. The size of a person's pupils can give you a definite clue as to how he or she is reacting to your ideas. Research shows that pupils dilate when persons react positively to what they hear or see, and constrict when their response is negative.

## AUDIENCE INVOLVEMENT

Consider: People are much more likely to be supportive of something they're made to feel a part of. Involving your audience is one of the smartest things you can do as a speaker to make your presentation a success.

## AUDIENCE ANALYSIS FORM

NAME OF GROUP _____

DATE _____

PLACE _____

TIME _____

SIZE OF AUDIENCE _____

LENGTH OF PRESENTATION _____

MAKEUP OF AUDIENCE (ETHNICITY,
SEX, EDUCATIONAL BACKGROUND,
INTERESTS, OCCUPATIONS, ETC.) _____

_____

_____

GROUP'S PURPOSE IN ASKING YOU TO SPEAK

_____

TOPIC OF SPEECH _____

HOW MUCH DOES AUDIENCE
KNOW ABOUT SUBJECT? _____

_____

WHAT IS THE AUDIENCE'S ATTITUDE TOWARD
SUBJECT? _____

WILL OTHER PRESENTATIONS BE GIVEN? _____

WILL A QUESTION-AND-ANSWER
PERIOD BE APPROPRIATE? _____

FEATURES OF MEETING ROOM _____

_____

ARRANGEMENTS FOR ANY A-V AIDS _____

AUDIENCE'S ATTITUDE TOWARD YOU
AND YOUR ORGANIZATION _____

SENSITIVE LOCAL TOPICS OR RECENT EVENTS _____

_____

_____

_____

Involving the listener in your presentation gives the impression that you care very much about communicating with him or her as an individual—that you're not just up there to talk to faceless forms and to hear your own voice. It also shows your professionalism in spending the time necessary to plan strategies to reach and involve that particular group.

As a result, your audience will feel included; an integral part of the presentation; and that the presentation was exactly tailored to fit that particular group.

There are many strategies you can use to get your audience significantly involved in what you're saying.

Look for their "trophy case"—something you can compliment them on. This could be an outstanding month of sales, a successfully completed community project of a service club, improved employee attendance, or whatever. Have those involved stand, and give them a hand. Or if the whole group participated in the accomplishment, have them applaud themselves.

Get them to give another round of applause for someone who has just finished performing—another speaker, the master of ceremonies, a singer. This not only involves the audience, it makes you look good when you give credit to someone else on the program.

Tell your listeners what's in it for them as individuals. Research has shown that people are most concerned about health, safety, and money. Try to appeal to those concerns.

Hit your audience's "hot button." Use an illustration about something that really turns them on, that they have a burning interest in.

Use examples, quotes, anecdotes about people you know the audience holds in high esteem and identifies with. In the case of a particular ethnic group, quote a leader, e.g., a congressman of that race. If you're speaking to a women's group, use an outstanding, successful woman as an example. Or talk about a person from their city or state.

Use the names of people in the audience. For example, you might say something like, "As a trial lawyer, I'm sure Sam can tell you the importance of learning to think on your feet." Mention something someone in the audience said that relates to your topic. Tell a story, even if it's hypothetical, about audience members. But either get their permission first or be *very sure* they will not be embarrassed and will enjoy the reference.

Show concern for your audience's comfort and convenience. If it seems to be getting too warm, ask how many are uncomfortable and request that the thermostat be adjusted.

Get and maintain good eye contact with listeners in various sections of the audience.

Use the pronoun "you" a lot. Talk about "we." Reveal something about yourself. "Confess" that you have that same problem, or whatever. This bridges the distance between the podium and the seats and builds bonds of friendship.

Humor is an excellent means of involvement. Sharing a good laugh makes everyone feel warm and friendly.

Have audience members raise their hands. Ask questions like, "How many of you are native Dallasites?" or Baptists or whatever. Or ask a piercing question such as "How many of you have ever felt like leaving your spouse?" and then, very quickly say, "No, don't answer that question."

Have members of the audience stand or the whole audience stand—particularly if they seem to be getting drowsy in a hot, crowded room.

Have the audience repeat together a key word or key phrase you're discussing.

Have listeners turn to a neighbor and tell them an important statement you want to emphasize.

Say that what you are going to tell them next is very important.

Give your listeners a mental task to perform. For example, ask them to think of their biggest problem and how what you just said relates to it. See if someone would like to share this with the audience.

At a certain point, dramatically remove an article of clothing, such as shoes, coat, or tie. For example, a school superintendent got the audience in the palm of his hand when he talked to administrators about the importance of seeing everything through the eyes of the classroom teacher. He took off his coat when he told of going back to the classroom and teaching a class every day himself so he could get back in touch with the challenges and problems teachers face day-to-day.

Give the audience a brief quiz on your subject either before or after the main part of your speech. You can ask for a show of hands or elicit individual responses from the audience.

Divide the audience into small buzz groups and have a reporter from each group share the responses with the whole group. This is excellent for use in a workshop-type presentation or when you have been given a very long time for your presentation.

Ask the audience for individual responses and write them on a chalkboard or flip chart. For example, you might ask, "What happens to you when you have stage fright?"

Give them a carefully prepared handout—one they will not just sit and read while you're talking. It can be one in which they fill in certain blanks, based on what you're covering.

Give them group exercises to perform. For example, in a presentation on listening, you could have them divide into pairs and talk to each other about their favorite subject at the same time and see how much they learn.

Give them hands-on practice. For example, in a presentation on letter writing, give them a hypothetical situation and ask them to write a letter based on what you've covered.

Hold a question-and-answer session. Tell the audience near the beginning of your speech that you're going to have a Q & A session. This will motivate them to keep track of what you're saying and will give them time to think of a good question on the subject.

Physically invade the territory of your audience. Going out into the audience with purpose can really get people involved.

Use audience members to stage an impromptu drama to illustrate your point. For example, a minister had a young man lie down on a bench on the platform and portray Isaac on the altar while he acted out the part of Abraham as he started to kill his son.

Take an instant poll of your audience by giving them different colored pieces of cardboard. You could use blue for a yes response and red for a no response, for example, or three colors for a multiple choice question. Ask them to hold up their choice and have assistants tally the response. Then give them the results.

Use your imagination to lead your audience to a response. The possibilities are really limitless.

Involving your audience is worth every bit of the effort and planning that it requires. But you can easily turn them off—if you're not careful.

## "LAUGH AND THE WORLD LAUGHS WITH YOU"

"Laughter is not at all a bad beginning for a friendship."[1]—Oscar Wilde

"Laughs are therapeutic. They soothe, heal and build relationships, and give an audience the chance to break the tension of the moment and draw back to absorb and rethink what you're saying."[2]—Bob Orben

"Wit is a sword; it is meant to make people feel the point as well as see it."[3]—G. K. Chesterton

"Wit ought to be a glorious treat, like caviar; never spread it about like marmalade."[4]—Sir Noel Coward

"Laugh at yourself first, before anyone else can."[5]—Elsa Maxwell

"A merry heart doeth good like medicine; but a broken spirit drieth the bones."—Proverbs 17:22

## HUMOR

Consider: Getting your audience to laugh is one of the quickest and most effective ways to establish rapport and to create a warm, responsive atmosphere. But dangers lurk therein. Humor must be used judiciously and with caution.

What is humor? Roger P. Wilcox says that humor depends on three elements: incongruity, suddenness or surprise, followed by a sense of well-being. He goes on to explain that humor is when two things which do not normally go together, suddenly and unexpectedly are found together and "when somehow we can retain a sense of relative well-being with regard to it."[6]

Alan H. Monroe lists seven different kinds of humor.

1.  Exaggeration, overstatement.
2.  Puns—using words which have a double meaning or which sound like other words with a different meaning.

3.  Poking fun at dignity or someone in authority.
4.  Irony—saying something in such a way that the opposite meaning is obviously implied.
5.  Burlesque—treating absurd things seriously or serious things absurdly.
6.  Unexpected turns—leading your audience to believe that you are going to say the normal thing and then saying just the opposite.
7.  Idiosyncrasies of people.[7]

Bob Orben, known as the dean of American comedy writers and writer for such notables as Jack Paar, Red Skelton, and Dick Gregory, says humor is, "Probably the strongest, most flexible, most humanizing device to bridge the space between speaker and audience."[8]

Humor creates interest and attention. It makes the speaker appear more human and gets the audience in the speaker's camp. Telling a joke on yourself is a great rapport builder.

---

## THINGS THAT TURN LISTENERS OFF

1.  A know-it-all attitude
2.  Talking down to an audience . . . or talking way over their heads
3.  Using too-big words, acronyms, and terminology they aren't familiar with
4.  Overpersuasion, overselling . . . the speaker who clobbers the audience
5.  A woman trying to act like "one of the boys"
6.  A speaker who smokes or drinks coffee or a cold drink while speaking
7.  Repetitious movements such as rocking, pacing, etc.
8.  A speaker blocking the view of visual material
9.  Profanity and smutty material
10.  Speaker playing with pencil, mike cord, etc.
11.  Putdowns of audience or any group of people
12.  A speaker who cannot be easily heard

Humor should be relevant to your subject. A humorous story or a joke should move your message forward, not take the audience's attention away from the subject. Don't tell a joke just because you think it is a good story or will get a laugh. What if it doesn't? Then you're stuck in an awkward situation. When a joke that's on the subject doesn't get a laugh, you can always say, "The reason I mentioned that story is . . ." and continue on with your speech.

It should be in good taste. The bottom line when you tell a joke is not "Did you get a laugh?" but "Did you get a laugh without offending your audience?" A good rule of thumb to follow is: "When in doubt, leave it out." Avoid—at all costs—any ethnic jokes or jokes that put down one sex or a group of people, such as a race, handicapped people, a trade, or profession. Remember:

Speak no evil and cause no ache;
Utter no jest that can pain awake;
Guard your actions and bridle your tongue;
Words are adders when hearts are stung.[9]

Be sure that the jokes and stories belong to you. No matter what the source, make them your own by adding personal touches, using your own language. It should match your personality, your style.

Make the story sound like it really happened—even if it didn't. Telling about your own job interview or about someone's in the audience makes it more interesting and believable than talking about a faceless blob.

Localize your humor. If the joke takes place in a hotel lobby, place it in the hotel where you're meeting or one that's well known—a place your listeners can visualize and identify with.

Be aware that receptivity to humor increases as the day goes on. Breakfast is tough. Lunch is o.k. Dinner is good. After dinner is best. "People are done with the cares of the day, and they're ready for a laugh," Orben points out.[10]

Know your audience. You have to know where their heads are. What's their general educational level? How sophisticated or blase are they? What's their age? What's their general socio-economic level?

Let your humor be an extension of yourself as a person, in keeping with your personality.

Don't laugh at your own jokes. You may be doing a solo.

Don't try to explain a joke if it falls flat. If it needs explaining, you never should have told it in the first place.

Look for humor in real life. Some of the funniest, most entertaining stories come from everyday experience.

Avoid stories that are long and drawn out.

Humor can be used effectively—even if your subject is very serious. In fact, a very heavy topic probably needs the leaven of at least a few smiles or chuckles.

Just as a spoonful of sugar helps the medicine go down, a dose of humor can make a controversial or hard message more palatable to the listener. For example, in a sales meeting where sales are down due to an apparent lack of initiative, making a humorous comparison can be much more effective than beating the listeners over the head with words of reproach.

Tie humor to major points in your speech. People will often remember a funny story long after they've forgotten the rest. Capitalize on this and let humor put across your premise.

Sprinkle humor at intervals throughout the speech. There's nothing like a good laugh to keep people alert and awake.

Tell your joke several times to two or three people before trying it out on an audience.

Know your stories backward and forward. It's not likely you'll get a laugh if you read a joke.

Realize that it is more difficult to get an audience to respond with laughter in an outdoor setting. Laughter is contagious and is lost outdoors.

Hearing someone else laugh encourages others to laugh. It also can encourage you as a speaker, get you on "a roll" so that you become funnier and funnier.

Getting people to laugh is great. But what if you simply cannot tell a joke? Don't try. If you can't get a few friends to laugh at your jokes, you certainly don't want to face the deadly silence of an audience that's supposed to laugh and doesn't. Instead, try humor. Almost everyone can handle a humorous story even if they can't get a laugh with a joke. And remember, humor doesn't have to have people doubled over in laughter. Even a quiet smile or a soft chuckle is enjoyable to your audience.

Timing is the critical factor in getting a laugh. While it

seems that some people are just born with a good sense of timing—pausing at the right moment, speeding up, slowing down—most of us have to work to develop that particular skill. Study professional comedians, observe how they do it, and learn from them.

Also, don't be afraid to ham it up. Acting out a story adds a lot. For instance, if it's a story with two different characters, assume a different stance, facial expression, and body position. For one character, turn slightly to the left; for the other, slightly to the right. Become a thespian. It will add life to your story.

Don't forget to use humor. All of us need its uplifting power. If nothing else, it gives the audience a chance to get together on something. Laughter is a community activity and provides a potent bond with others.

Remember, humor is as essential to a good talk as seasoning is to a good meal.

## THE QUESTION-AND-ANSWER SESSION

Consider: Most speeches are not complete without a question-and-answer period.

Many speakers do a superb job of delivering the formal presentation, then ruin the whole thing by poorly handling questions from the audience.

### Some Do's

Treat the question-and-answer period as a part of the speech. The speech is not over until the last question is answered and the speaker sits down.

It is embarrassing to ask for questions and have none asked because of the reluctance on the part of audience members to ask the first question. A good technique for "priming the pump" when this happens is to say, "A question I am frequently asked is ..." and then answer that question. Often that's all that's needed to get the questions flowing.

Look directly at the person asking the question. Show total interest in that person and what is being asked. Keep your hands free.

Listen for both content and feeling by observing facial expressions and body language.

Repeat the question for the rest of the audience. If you're not sure exactly what the questioner means, paraphrase the question with, "Let me be sure I understand what you're asking."

Thank the questioner. Look at the entire audience while answering, glancing back occasionally to the person who asked the question.

If the question is emotionally charged or belligerent, show understanding of the person's position or feelings. Demonstrate that you value the questioner as a person even though your position may be quite different. Never put down the questioner or get in a verbal battle.

Treat two questions from the same person as two separate questions.

Admit you don't have an answer if you don't know. Offer to find out and get back to that person. Ask for the person's name and phone number and be sure to contact him or her later.

Be factual and accurate. Avoid phrases like "They say . . ." or "A recent report . . ." or "It is a well-known fact . . ."

Rotate the way you select questions from the audience. Let individuals seated in all areas of the room have a chance to speak.

Anticipate the kinds of questions you will be asked and have statistics, quotes, etc., at your fingertips.

Keep a positive attitude. Avoid getting on the defensive.

Remain in control of the session.

Do not let the question-and-answer session drag on or fizzle out. Be sure to keep it within the time limits set by the program chairman. When you're nearly out of time, tell your audience, "There's time for only one more question."

Keep your answers brief and to the point, but be sure to answer the question as completely as possible. A good format to follow in many cases is to give a one sentence answer or a "yes" or "no," give the reason, a brief example, and a restatement of your answer.

Save a clincher statement, a summary of your speech, or a dynamic ending to use at the end of your question-and-answer session rather than just mumbling "thank you" and trailing off after the last question.

Turn the complaint or non-question into a question. For example, if a member of the audience says, "We sure don't need any higher taxes," you can say, "I hear a very important question in your statement. Why should we pay any more taxes than we're already paying?" Then answer the question you've made up.

### Some Don'ts

Resist the temptation to gather up your notes and prepare to leave the speaker's stand while the first question is being asked. This makes the speaker appear to be not really interested in answering questions the audience might have.

Don't grade questions by telling one questioner, "That's a good question," but not telling others their questions are good, too. Just answer the question.

Don't allow one person to ask all the questions. Simply say, "Many others have questions. I'll get back to you if there is time."

Avoid answering with such phrases as "Well, obviously . . ." or "As I said in my talk . . ." or "Anyone should know the answer to that . . ." These are all put-down phrases.

Don't use negative body language. Don't put your hands on your hips or fold your arms over your chest while you're listening to the question or answering.

Don't point one finger at your audience while speaking. That's a scolding pose and makes you seem "preachy."

Avoid "off-the-record" statements.

Never hedge or avoid answering a question. Give them a straight answer.

Don't argue with the questioner. If he or she persists, offer to discuss the question with the person after the meeting.

Don't get down on the level of a nasty questioner. Usually the audience will take care of a rude member in its midst if you remain the "good guy."

Don't feel obligated to agree with the questioner if you actually disagree . . . but learn to disagree diplomatically.

# 5

# *Audio-Visual Approaches*

Consider: "When relying on verbalization alone to communicate, an estimated 90 percent of a message is misinterpreted or forgotten entirely. We retain only 10 percent of what we hear. Adding appropriate visual aids to verbalization increases retention to approximately 50 percent."[1]—3M How-To Guide

The use of audio-visual approaches to communicating is certainly no new thing. In fact, we might say the caveman was the first advocate of A-V. After all, he drew pictures on the walls of his cave to better express his thoughts and feelings.

There are many different audio-visual approaches. In fact, the most basic one is the speaker—his or her appearance, eye contact, facial expressions, gestures.

Then there are those that have been around a long time, such as the chalkboard and the flip chart.

Technology has ushered in a whole host of approaches that can be used effectively to add life and longevity to the speaker's words. In fact, there are so many choices, it can get confusing. Knowing which aid to use where and in what circumstances is vitally important. In fact, choosing the wrong aid, using it incorrectly, and having poorly prepared visuals can be distracting instead of enhancing to the presentation.

These are some general rules to keep in mind in the use of audio-visual aids. Remember the three B's. Visual material must be big, bold, and brilliant. Nothing is more irritating than to have a speaker refer to a visual that has print or detail too small to be seen.

A good visual standard to remember is:
- One idea per visual
- Six words per line
- Six lines per visual

Visual material should be kept simple. Probably the most common mistake is having too many visuals and trying to put too much information on each one.

• Check out your equipment and make sure it's working properly well in advance of the meeting. Always have extra bulbs at hand in case one burns out. If a projectionist is needed, be sure you have someone who really knows how to operate the equipment—not just the first person who volunteers. When using an aid, such as slides or overhead transparencies, be sure they are numbered in case they are dropped or have gotten out of order. Be sure to check to ensure that they are in the right order before the meeting begins.

• Make certain that the screen is located where everyone can easily see it. This may require rearranging the room, especially if there are posts involved. Be sure that the speaker will not block the screen when it is being used. Make sure the projectors are properly loaded and focused before the meeting begins.

• Check the volume level on audio equipment and set it properly in advance. A deafening roar at the beginning or an inaudible first minute of a presentation negates much of the potential effect.

• If lights need to be turned off and back on, have you assigned someone to do that very important function? Have you worked out in advance all necessary cues with others who are assisting with your presentation?

• Have someone proof your audio-visual material for errors and for clarity of meaning. Be sure that any material you use is sharp-looking. A sloppy visual makes a poor impression and is better tossed in the circular file.

• Practice your presentation if you have several pieces to manipulate.

• If several approaches and several people are involved, have a rehearsal beforehand to make sure everything is working properly and everyone understands what to do.

• Know how much time is required for using each aid and

be sure to include the required number of minutes in your overall presentation time.

• Be cautious about leaving the audience in a darkened room too long—especially after eating a large meal. You may hear several snores in the background.

• Place any aids you are going to operate near your speaking position. Avoid long treks to and from a chalkboard, etc. Do not speak toward your visual aid. Always be sure you are facing the audience. Be sure you're not blocking the view of any member of an audience. Stand by the side of a map or chart and use a pointer, holding it in the hand nearest the visual, to point out a certain area. In the case of an overhead transparency, use a pencil or pen on the stage of the projector to point out a certain area of the visual rather than going to the screen.

• Be sure the visual is kept up long enough for the viewer to grasp the contents of the visual. This is especially important if participants are taking notes. Don't forget to interact with your audience while using audio-visual approaches. While this is not possible with some media, such as a movie, other aids lend themselves to interaction and audience involvement.

• Audio-visual material is aptly called an aid. It should be used to help you communicate more effectively—not to do your job for you. Do not let your audio-visual aids overpower you. Remember, you're still the star of the show. You should not be upstaged.

• There are few things more irritating to an audience than audio-visual equipment that doesn't work or isn't operated correctly, and material that can't be seen or heard. Learn how to use it expertly or leave it out.

Selecting the best A-V aid to do a particular job is important. The information contained on the next few pages should help you in deciding on the most appropriate approach for your particular presentation.


## VISUAL AID: OVERHEAD PROJECTOR


**Advantages:**

• Transparencies can be used in a lighted room.

- Transparencies can be used with a rather large group of people.
- Speaker can operate projector and thus maintain complete control over the presentation.
- Speaker can face the audience and does not have to leave speaking area.
- Speaker can point out features on the transparency with a pen on the stage of the projector itself.
- Transparencies can be used periodically during the presentation by merely flipping on a switch.
- Prepared transparencies can be used with the information being revealed a line at a time when this is desirable.
- Information on a prepared transparency can be highlighted with a special pen during the presentation.
- Presenter can write on the transparency during presentation. Feedback from the audience can easily be recorded and projected for the whole group to see and consider.
- Transparencies are relatively inexpensive.
- Nice-looking transparencies can be made using a typewriter with large type and a copying machine—equipment that's usually accessible to most speakers.
- Overhead projectors can be equipped with a two-way acetate roll attachment allowing the speaker to use a continuous roll of acetate when this would be easier.

**Disadvantage:**

- Keystone effect of image will result unless projector and screen are carefully positioned.

**Tips:**

- Screen should be positioned at an angle behind and to the left or right of the speaker. Otherwise, the view of the listener will be blocked.
- Color highlight film can be used to good effect on portions of the transparency.
- Overlays can be effectively used in showing the parts of a whole, etc.
- Opaque background film gives a dramatic effect since it looks like the writing or drawing suddenly appeared.
- Beware of using the same repetitious pattern for too long a

period. It's a good idea to vary your presentation. For example, you might use two or three transparencies revealing a point at a time, then a transparency making a single point. Using transparencies throughout an entire presentation can become monotonous.

## VISUAL AID: OPAQUE PROJECTOR

**Advantages:**
- A picture, document, book, and some three-dimensional material may be projected.
- Most opaque projectors have an arrow or spot of light that may be positioned to point out a certain part of the picture or whatever is being projected.
- No processing or production of material is required.
- Pictures may be mounted on a long sheet of paper and moved through the projector with a roller.
- It may be used with a fairly large group of people.

**Disadvantages:**
- The room must be darkened.
- A projectionist must be used or the speaker must have his or her back to the audience in order to operate the equipment.
- The projector is large and not easily moved.
- The fan of the projector is comparatively noisy.
- The strong light may "blind" the audience when the projection stage is lowered.
- Because an opaque projector needs to be placed as close to the screen as possible, a rearrangement of seating may be necessary.

**Tips:**
- Great care should be exercised when using books in an opaque projector.
- The mechanics of getting the material in and out of the projector should be practiced in advance.

## AUDIO-VISUAL AID: MOTION PICTURE FILM

**Advantages:**

- The film can show movement.
- It can vicariously take the audience to another location, another time in history.
- It provides a common experience for the audience.
- It can serve as a launching pad for discussion.
- Many different types of film are available for rental at varying costs.
- Films may be shown to a very large group of people although additional speakers may be necessary in a large auditorium.

**Disadvantages:**

- Room must be darkened.
- A professional projectionist is necessary.
- Speaker loses rapport with audience since as a rule the film is self-contained and the speaker cannot interact.

**Tips:**

- Projector should never be left to run alone.
- The film should be carefully introduced to prepare the viewer for what is important, of particular interest to that group, etc.
- Highlights of the film should be summarized afterwards.
- The film may be used as an excellent vehicle to launch a group discussion.

## VISUAL AID: SLIDE PROJECTOR

**Advantages:**

- Slides can be used with a large audience.
- With a carousel projector and remote control, speaker can operate equipment.
- Speaker can dwell as long as desired on one particular slide.

- Slide presentations can be easily changed and varied to meet the interest and appropriateness of a certain audience or occasion.

**Disadvantage:**

- The room must be darkened or nearly darkened.

**Tips:**

- Cardboard frames on slides are safer than plastic ones which will sometimes warp when they get hot in the projector.
- The speaker should stand to the right of the screen (audience's left). Since we read from right to left, this is a stronger position for maintaining audience attention.
- A light on the lectern will be needed if the speaker must use notes during the slide presentation.
- A cordless remote slide changer may be purchased, which gives the speaker a great deal more freedom of movement.
- Pace the slide show to maintain audience interest. Keeping one slide on the screen for too long invites audience members' minds to drift. As a rule, six to eight slides per minute will maintain attention.
- Limit the length of the slide show to about ten minutes—fifteen at the very most.
- Don't give in to the temptation to use a nearly good slide. Select only those that are top quality and have something to say.
- Check to be sure the slides are loaded properly. An upside down shot or one with the letters running backwards puts a damper on the whole presentation.

## AUDIO-VISUAL AID: TELEVISION

**Advantages:**

- TV can be used in a lighted room.
- Many video cassette tapes on a variety of subjects are now available.

- The equipment can be easily stopped and started to call attention to a certain point.
- Television is particularly helpful in training situations, such as for public speaking, since feedback can be immediate.
- Material may be edited with proper equipment.
- The price of good television equipment is going down.
- Television shows motion and is good for demonstrations and for showing up close an object the audience could not otherwise see.

**Disadvantage:**

- Television cannot be effectively used with a large group of people unless a very large screen is rented. This runs several hundred dollars for rental and is only available in the larger cities.

**Tip:**

- If you have a pretty good-sized audience, use more than one receiver, located for optimum viewing.

## AUDIO AID: AUDIO TAPE RECORDER

**Advantages:**

- Audio tapes are inexpensive and easy to use.
- A speaker can back up a point of view with "the expert" on the subject.
- Music or recorded sounds may be used to illustrate or dramatize a point.
- Music can be used effectively to stimulate, soothe, or set the mood for a particular presentation, or to change the emotional climate during a presentation.
- Pre-recorded dialogue may be used to spark discussion or as an example.
- The tape recorder may be used effectively in training when the spoken word is important.

**Disadvantages:**

- Care must be taken that all audience members can hear the recording.

- The audience may lose interest with nothing to watch if the tape is very long.

**Tip:**

- Don't overlook the audio recorder as a possibility to add color and life to your presentation.

## VISUAL AID: CHALKBOARD

**Advantages:**

- Key points and words can be easily and spontaneously emphasized.
- Responses from the audience can be listed and referred to.
- Material can be erased and board reused immediately.

**Disadvantages:**

- Chalkboards cannot be used effectively with a large group.
- The audience's attention may be easily lost as the speaker writes with his or her back to the audience.
- Chalkboards are difficult to position so that the entire group can readily see them.
- When the chalkboard is used repeatedly, the chalk residue makes writing progressively more difficult to read.

**Tips:**

- Be sure the writing is large enough to be easily read from the back row. With a viewing distance from the chalkboard of thirty-two feet, lettering should be at least 2½ inches high.
- Limit your writing to key words or phrases.
- While you write do not remain with your back to the audience for more than a few seconds at a time.
- If information is written in advance of the presentation, be sure the chalkboard is turned around or covered. Otherwise, the audience will read instead of listening to the speaker.
- Black chalkboards are more legible than green ones.
- If a chalkboard is used over and over, see that it is washed

with a damp cloth during breaks to ensure greater legibility.
- Once you have written on the chalkboard, get away from it. This is important so that you don't block the listener's view and also so that you don't succumb to the temptation to "fiddle" with the board
- Use a pointer rather than your hand if you wish to emphasize certain written information.
- Erase the chalkboard when you are finished using it. Otherwise, the written information will be distracting.

## VISUAL AID: FLIP CHART

**Advantages:**
- Flip charts are relatively inexpensive.
- Material can be prepared in advance, using color in drawings, graphs, and charts.
- Key points and words can be easily and spontaneously emphasized.
- Responses from audience can be listed and referred to.

**Disadvantages:**
- Flip charts cannot be used effectively with a large group.
- It is easy to lose your audience's attention if you write with your back to the audience for too long a period of time.

**Tips:**
- Use a blank sheet as you begin your presentation.
- Place blank sheets between pre-prepared sheets so that you may cover your message when you are speaking on a different subject.
- Be sure the writing is large enough (and thick enough) to be easily read from the back row.
- Limit your writing to key words or phrases.
- While you write do not remain with your back to the audience for more than a few seconds at a time.
- Practice turning the sheets until it becomes easy and second nature.
- Once you have written on the sheet or turned to the next

page, move away from the chart.
- Use a pointer rather than your hand if you wish to emphasize certain written information or a part of a chart or graph.
- Be sure not to block the view of the audience.
- If you prepare charts in advance, be sure to have someone else proof them for errors.
- Know the material on your charts so you don't have to read from them and end up with a swivel head from looking back and forth at them and at your audience.

## VISUAL AID: FLANNEL, HOOK-AND-LOOP, AND MAGNET BOARDS

**Advantages:**
- Drawings or work of the group may be easily displayed.
- Materials such as cloth, yarn, bits of balsa wood, blotting paper, and sponge will adhere to a flannel board. Hook-and-loop boards allow objects to be firmly attached yet instantly removed or manipulated. Odd-shaped and heavy objects (up to several pounds) may also be attached. Small metal objects will adhere to a magnet board and magnets may be used to hold thin objects of paper or cloth.
- An idea presentation may be built, piece by piece, in an orderly sequence.
- Members of the audience may be involved by asking them to regroup or reposition the objects for a specific reason.
- These boards may be used effectively in teaching a group how to play a particular sport, game, or skill.

**Disadvantage:**
- Magnet, hook-and-loop, and flannel boards cannot be used effectively with a large group.

**Tips:**
- Presentations with magnet, hook-and-loop, and flannel boards should be kept simple.

- A flannel board should be tilted very slightly back at the top to help materials stick firmly to the flannel surface.
- Be sure to step aside after applying the picture or object to the board's surface so as not to block the audience's line of vision.
- Have a conveniently close working surface available to store visual material before use.
- Check order of visual material and be sure it is separated for easy handling.

## VISUAL AID: MODELS AND OBJECTS

**Advantages:**

- Models and objects are good attention-getters and can add realism to a presentation.
- Visual aids that actually do something during the speech are especially interesting.
- The three-dimensional aspect gives them a distinct advantage over pictures.
- Models and objects can usually be handled by the audience, giving a kinesthetic dimension to the presentation.

**Disadvantage:**

- Models and objects cannot be used effectively with a large group unless they are very big.

**Tips:**

- The object or model should be concealed until the time for its discussion in your presentation. Otherwise, it will be distracting.
- If it is impossible to let everyone in the group manipulate the object or model during the presentation, provide an opportunity for the others after you are finished.
- Be sure the object or model is positioned high enough so that those seated on the back row will be able to see it.
- Even something too small to be seen can be used effectively if you want to show just how small it really is.
- Let your imagination run riot in coming up with ideas for the use of real-life objects. For example, a former secre-

tary of agriculture used slices from a real loaf of bread to show the percentage of profit the farmer, the baker, and the retailer receive.

## VISUAL AID: HANDOUTS

**Advantages:**
- Handouts can be used advantageously to involve listeners in the presentation by giving them a certain graph or chart to look at, or a quiz to take.
- Handouts can reinforce the presentation later and can be valuable for future reference.

**Disadvantage:**
- Handouts can become so absorbing to the audience that it is difficult for the speaker to get members to look at the podium.

**Tips:**
- Be sure to make arrangements with enough helpers to get the material handed out quickly, quietly, and efficiently.
- Be certain to have more than enough copies available for those present. Audience members become very irritated if they don't get a handout—even if they don't particularly want one.
- If the handout is the same as your presentation, do not hand it out until after the presentation. Above all, don't stand up and read the handout aloud to your audience.
- Unless following the handout is important to your presentation, wait until after you finish to distribute it. Otherwise, people have a tendency to sit and read instead of listening to what you're saying.
- If you prepare the material yourself, be sure to have someone else proof the final copy.
- Make sure the reproduction is top quality. A barely legible or ink-smeared copy makes a negative statement about you as a speaker.
- Handout materials should have the name of the material and the speaker's or author's name on each page.

# AUDIO AID: MICROPHONE

**Advantages:**

- Voice can be amplified to ensure audibility.
- A lavaliere microphone gives the speaker greater flexibility, with a cordless mike providing the maximum ease of movement.
- In a relatively large area, the speaker can speak very softly for effect without worrying about being heard.

**Disadvantages:**

- Unless excellent equipment is available, voice can be distorted.
- Use of a stationary mike limits movement of speaker.
- A hand-held mike limits effectiveness of gestures.
- Microphones magnify speech defects, such as a hissing sound or smacking of lips.
- Feedback can be very disconcerting to an audience. Correct positioning and operation are essential.

**Tips:**

- Speaker should try out the mike before the meeting begins and get the level set. Realize that a full auditorium will change the sound and the level will probably need to be adjusted.
- Speaker should be certain to know how to turn the mike on and adjust the height of the stand.
- Speaker must be adept at using a mike effectively—backing away when getting louder and getting closer when softer.
- Speaker must realize that he or she cannot really tell how the voice sounds to the audience and must rely on the sound technician to make necessary adjustments.
- Speaker should not substitute the use of a microphone for good projection techniques.
- Speaker must be aware that feedback can result if the mike is placed too close to other sound equipment such as speakers and other microphones.

## AUDIO-VISUAL CHECKLIST

Have you checked out the meeting room or the auditorium to be sure of any adaptive measures and their availability, such as use of extension cords, means of darkening room, special stands, etc., that will be needed to use certain A-V approaches?

Have you allowed plenty of time for setting up and checking out A-V equipment?

Have you checked several days in advance of the engagement to be certain all equipment is in good working order?

Do you have the equipment in place and in the most advantageous position?

Have you placed electrician's tape over any extension cords where people may be walking?

Have you focused any projectors you might be using?

Have you cued up any tapes or films so that there will be no awkward pause when they are turned on?

Have you made arrangements with someone to turn off and on the lights (if necessary) on a certain cue?

Have you concealed any A-V material you will be using in a manner that will be easy to unmask at the proper time?

Have you tested the level of any sound equipment you plan to use, including a microphone?

Have you checked out the visibility of your material from all parts of the meeting area?

Have you made arrangements with a competent projectionist to turn on and off the equipment on cue and make certain it is working properly if you cannot operate it yourself?

Do you have spare bulbs on hand in case the one in your projector burns out?

Do you have your slides, transparencies, or other material numbered, and have you checked to make sure they are in the proper order?

Have you practiced using your A-V aids to make certain you can handle them smoothly and professionally?

## KEEP IT SIMPLE, SPEAKER

There's an old formula, the KISS formula, that public speakers would profit from taking to heart . . . and that is to keep it simple.

They also would do well to heed an old country preacher's formula for a good sermon.

"Tell them what you're going to tell them.

Tell them.

Tell them what you told them."

In the beginning—

     —grab their interest

        In the middle—

            —expand their understanding

                In the end—

                    —reinforce and cap it off

Like a gamefish, a speech needs:

a head . . .

a connecting spine with plenty of muscular support . . .

                    and a tail.[2]

# 6

# *Writing the Speech*

Consider: Some years ago the British House of Commons was interrupted by the news that the cable to Africa had been completed. After the huzzahs and hat tossing had died down, Winston Churchill rose to say, "Excellent. Excellent. Now, what shall we *tell* the Africans?"[1]

You've been asked to speak. You've accepted. Now, what will you *tell* your audience?

Someone has said that "An agreement to make a speech may be compared with a pregnancy. Only as the day of delivery draws near does the full realization of the magnitude of your commitment to deliver hit you."[1]

As a speaker, sometimes you will be given a specific topic or a general subject to speak on. Other times you will be told to talk about whatever you want to. Regardless of which option you are given, it will be up to you to determine exactly what approach you will take, just how broad or narrow to make the subject, and how you will make it specifically apply to and interest the audience you will be addressing.

## THE TITLE

While it is not always necessary to give your speech a title, often you will be asked several weeks in advance to provide a title for use in publicizing your presentation or for a printed program. An intriguing title can be an effective interest-piquer and stage setter in the remarks of the person who introduces you. You can also use it as a continuity phrase in the body of your speech to remind your listeners of your subject.

Here are some suggestions to keep in mind in deciding on a title.

Keep it short. Consider how it will look in the program.

Try to make it interest-grabbing for that particular group.

Be sure it really says what you're going to be talking about.

Make it catchy. Toy with words and try to come up with something that has a nice "ring" to it. Consider alliteration or a play on words.

Be sure the mood of the title sets the tone for the speech. For example, you would not want to give a formal-sounding title to a fluffy, entertaining speech.

Say the title aloud and see how it sounds when spoken.

Bounce it off a few people whose opinions you respect.

Try using a provocative question.

Think of the title as a one-sentence summary or the essence of your entire speech.

## THE OBJECTIVE OF YOUR SPEECH

A top priority for you as a speaker is to decide your purpose for making this particular speech. What do you hope to do for (or to) your audience? There are six main objectives a speaker may adopt for a presentation.

1. To stimulate the audience, to persuade them to a particular point of view at an emotional level.
2. To convince the listener, to convey truth through a factual, logical approach.
3. To actuate the hearers, to get them to make a commitment to take action.
4. To inform the audience by presenting facts from an unbiased viewpoint.
5. To entertain the crowd in a non-persuasive, light-hearted presentation.
6. To inspire the listener to a broader perspective, a more humanitarian viewpoint, a nobler purpose.

You may have only one of the above objectives . . . or you may combine more than one objective. For example, your purpose may include persuading your audience to adopt a certain viewpoint, and then motivate them to a certain course of action.

Once you have determined your purpose, then the question is how do you write a speech? Where do you begin? How do you go about constructing an interesting, attention-keeping presentation? Basically there are four main parts to a well-constructed presentation: the introduction, the statement of purpose, the body, and the conclusion. While it may seem like the tail wagging the dog, probably the most carefully thought out and written part of your speech should be the introduction.

## THE INTRODUCTION

Your very first remarks are critical to the success of your entire presentation. Research has shown that you only have four minutes to prove yourself as a speaker. It's in those opening moments that the audience decides whether or not to listen to what you have to say.

Since that is the case, it is usually best to skip all perfunctory remarks about the weather and such. There are exceptions, if you used to be a member of the group you're addressing and you haven't seen the people in a long time, of course you would greet them and perhaps reminisce for a few seconds.

As a rule, though, you will want to begin with a real interest-grabber—something that will pique your listeners' curiosity or imagination and get them interested in what you have to say. You want to begin with force, not tentatively. It's very important for you to take charge as a speaker from the very first.

There are several approaches you can effectively use to get your audience's interest.

### The Startling Statement

Begin with something that will really make your listeners wonder what on earth you're talking about. For example, a speech on the violence shown on television might begin:

"Last night there were three rapes, five muggings, and seven murders in my next door neighbor's living room. Shocking? The really shocking thing is that the same thing was happening in homes throughout this nation. No one called the police. In fact, few people thought anything about allowing rapists, terrorists, and murderers to come in and talk with their children.

"Certainly we would risk our very lives to keep someone from giving one of our youngsters poison, and yet we, as American citizens, have permitted television masquerading as entertainment to poison the minds and sensibilities of this nation's most precious resource day after day, year after year."

## The Provocative Question

Ask a rhetorical question. Then pause and give your audience time to answer it. For example, a speech about the worth of the individual and each person's uniqueness and importance could start:

"Do you ever wonder who you are?

"To the post office you are 'occupant'.

"The bank lists you as 2-1273-04-50.

"To Southwestern Bell Telephone you are 214-555-3675.

"Do you ever feel like a prisoner in a world of statistics?

"A number? A part of a machine?

"Do you ever feel like saying, 'When I die, lay me away gently. Do not fold, bend, spindle, or mutilate me?'

"I say to you that you are not just a number or a statistic. Rather than feeling that way, I hope you'll be more like the student whose teacher asked him what of great importance is here today that did not exist twenty years ago. The young man promptly answered, 'Me!'"

## Humor that Makes a Point

Getting an audience to laugh is a good way to warm them up to you as a speaker. For example, here's a possible opener for a speech about the future.

"When we think about the future, sometime I think we're like the little old lady who went to the post office to mail a package. She asked the clerk to weigh the package for fear she hadn't used enough stamps. The clerk weighed it and then told her she had actually used too many.

"She said, 'Oh, dear. I do hope it won't go too far.'

"Well, I think we're a lot like that about the future. We read books such as *Future Shock* and *Megatrends*. We feel like gritting our teeth and just hoping against hope that the future won't go too far."

## The Analogy

Show how the group, the problem, the subject under discussion is like something the listener can easily relate to. For example, this makes a good beginning for a speech on leadership qualities:

"This morning I would like to ask you a question. Are you a thermometer or are you a thermostat? There's a vast difference.

"You see, when a room is cold, the mercury in the tube of a thermometer drops. When the room is warm, it rises. The thin red line adjusts itself automatically to the temperature of the room.

"Ah, but the thermostat works quite differently. No sooner does a room become cold than it sends a message to the furnace saying, 'Send up more heat.' When the room is too warm, it calls down, 'Enough. Stop for a while.'

"Thermometer people are followers. They merely react to what's going on around them. Thermostat people are proactive rather than reactive. They mold or shape the atmosphere around them. They take a given situation and take charge of it, giving it the direction and thrust that's needed."

## The Object

Use your imagination to come up with props that will immediately grab your audience's interest.

This introduction can be used for a speech on the importance of seeing the opportunities in any given situation, rather than just the problems.

(Speaker holds up a large piece of white cardboard with a black dot in the lower left hand corner.)

"What do you see?" (Get the audience to answer. Almost everyone will say "a black dot." Then ask this question and get them to respond by raising their hands.)

"How many of you saw a black dot?

"Of course, you could have seen a large, empty white space—big enough, in fact, to copy Lincoln's Gettysburg Address, the Ten Commandments, or the Bill of Rights.[2]

"A lot depends on our point of view."

### Reference to a Movie or Play

Set the scene and use a quote from a familiar movie or play. This example provides a provocative opener for a speech about the importance of working together.

"This wonderful occasion this evening reminds me of a bit of dialogue in the movie *Oh, God.*

"Those of you who saw the movie will recall that God, played by George Burns, tells Jerry Landers that the reason he decided to return at that particular time was because he made the world to work. Jerry immediately tells him: 'Well, if you've read the papers lately, it's not working. Why don't you do something about it?'

"God reminds him: 'Why don't you do something about it? It's your world.'

"Jerry says: 'But we need help.'

"And God replies: 'That's why I gave you each other.'[3]

"I believe that. We were given each other to help one another and to do together through cooperation what would simply be impossible to achieve through our own individual efforts."

### The Anecdote

People are always interested in a good, well-told story. Allan M. Laing said, "For most public speakers, anecdotes are the plums in the oratorical pudding; without them the average audience goes away nourished, perhaps, but not exhilarated."[4]

The following anecdote would set the stage nicely for a graduation speech.

"It was a foggy, dreary night. As Johnathon West approached the musty old cemetery, his feeling of uneasiness mounted. He had bragged once too often: 'I'm not scared of anything.' So here he was walking on hesitant feet among crumbling tombstones which cast strange shadows in the pale moonlight. He had to! It was either take the dare or lose face with his companions.

"Suddenly, he lurched forward and fell helplessly in a heap. He had fallen into a freshly dug grave. In a state of panic, he tried time and again to get out of the hole. He tried to walk up the sides. He tried to claw his way up. With all his might, he tried to jump out of the hole, but the sides were just too steep.

After exhausting himself with attempts to escape his eerie prison, he finally pulled his coat over him, lay down in one corner of the grave, and fell asleep. After a while he was awakened by a strange-sounding cry. And the next thing he knew he was no longer alone in the grave. In an instant, Johnathon jumped to his feet, leaped out of the grave in one bound, and didn't stop running until he got home.

"The difference was incentive. It was impossible for Johnathon to get out of the grave, and yet given a strong incentive, he accomplished what he had decided was impossible.

"What a difference incentive made for Johnathon. And what a difference it can make for you."

### A Children's Story or Rhyme

There's a lot of good speech material in children's stories. Have you read *Alice in Wonderland*, or *Winnie the Pooh*? If not, get out your old storybooks or visit the library to discover just how much depth and philosophy so-called children's stories contain.

Here's an example of a speech about reduction in force that starts with a child's verse.

"Our topic today—'Reductions in Force: Effective Decisions and Personnel Policies'—makes me think of an old childhood rhyme. Perhaps you remember it.

As I was going up the stairs,
I met a man who wasn't there.
He wasn't there again today;
Oh, how I wish he'd go away.

"Now the reason it makes me think of our topic is that the students who aren't there bring about the necessity for having to deal eventually with cutting staff, and I guess all of us would really like for the problem to just go away."

### The Gimmick

Think of some cute or folksy approach to get your audience's attention. For example, a speech on leadership could be built around the three Z's with each point being built on a word starting with a Z.

"My first Z is zoom.
"My next Z is zeal.
"My last Z is zest."

### The News Story

Excellent speech material can be found by being on the lookout for stories about real people in the newspaper or on the ten o'clock news. This real story about Mabel Schoonover made a good analogy with public education.

"Sometimes it seems like the public schools have an awful lot to overcome. In fact, sometimes public education reminds me of Mabel Schoonover of Floral City, Florida.

"It seems that seventy-year-old Mabel Schoonover was declared dead, bureaucratically by Medicare. It all started when she got a letter addressed to 'The Estate of M. Schoonover.' This is how she described her experience.

"'They told me in Jacksonville that it was a mistake. I told them I knew that already and they said it was the computer. I told the social security office that those idiots in Jacksonville have me dead. They assured me it would be sixty days before they could get me alive and I said it didn't take sixty days to get me dead.'

"Finally, the bureaucracy returned her from limbo to full life in early September.

"Well, the reason that Mabel makes me think of the public schools is I think we've already been declared dead or at least dying by a lot of people. In fact, I think some of the prophets of doom have already held the funeral and are just waiting for the lid to be closed on the casket.

"Now Mabel may have varicose veins, high blood pressure, and a touch of arthritis, but she's a long way from kicking the bucket. And so is public education."

### Quote a Famous Person, an Authority, or the Results of a Study

Quoting an expert or the conclusion of a study on your subject lends weight to your words.

This speech, "Women as Leaders," begins with the results of a study.

"Want to be the chief executive officer of a great American corporation?

"Be born in the Middle West. Go to college in the East. and be—if at all possible—a man.

"That's the message of a study on chief executives conducted by the executive-recruiting firm of Arthur Young Executive Resource Consultants involving 800 business leaders. One person associated with the study concludes flatly that the odds favor a woman being elected President of the United States before one becoming a chief executive officer of any of the top 500 U.S. industrial companies.

"No major corporation is known to have asked an executive research firm specifically to find a female chief executive. Katherine Graham, who took over the chairmanship of The Washington Post Co. after the death of her husband, is the only woman major corporation head in the U.S.

"The population inside the executive ranks is estimated at less than one percent female. At this time, there just aren't many women cast in that role.

"In other words, things haven't changed too much since Shakespeare's days. He didn't write many good parts for women either. And most of the women he did include didn't turn out too well. Lady Macbeth was a murderer. Desdemona was killed by her jealous husband, and Ophelia committed suicide.

"One of Shakespeare's heroines did fare somewhat better. This was Portia in *The Merchant of Venice* who saved the merchant's life with her clever arguments. But, of course, to be acceptable to the audiences of Shakespeare's time, Portia had to be disguised as a man. The result is an interesting paradox—reluctant acceptance and, on the other hand, known ability.

"Of course, I don't need to tell you that that analogy extends from the boundaries of stage to the real life status that society has accorded females for a long, long time."

## The Cartoon

Good cartoons have a way of quickly and concisely making a sharp point. They sometimes can be described very effectively as an opener. This was the beginning of a speech for the American Indian Symposium.

"A few years ago, *The New Yorker* published a cartoon showing an Indian father sitting inside his tepee reading a bedtime story to his son. The particular line he read was: 'And just then, when it appeared that the battle was lost, from beyond the hills came the welcome sound of war whoops.'

"Well, it was an amusing cartoon, but as humor often does, it made a very pointed and provocative statement. A great deal of how you view the world depends on whether you see salvation as fifty people wearing loincloths and feathers or fifty people wearing cavalry blue.

"This same cultural difference helps determine how you view the schools—and how the schools view you."

## The Hypothetical Story

Take the facts and statistics and make up a story about a particular, but imaginary, person that exemplifies your point. In other words, put flesh and feet on your facts. Your audience will be much more interested in hearing about a believable person than about a string of statistics.

This was the opening of a speech about the church's responsibility to minister to and meet the needs of the community.

"Cindy Cassidy is a six-year-old first grader at O.M. Roberts Elementary School in Dallas. An attractive child . . . somewhat shy and small for her age. She arrives at her apartment at 2:30 p.m., looks furtively all around, in every direction. She then takes the key from her tiny purse, unlocks the door, and goes inside.

"First, she makes sure the door is securely locked and checks out the layout of the small apartment. Then she calls her mother at work and reports that she's arrived home safely before settling down to watch TV at a low volume.

"There's a knock on the door. She sits motionless . . . scarcely breathing until she hears the footsteps fade away into the distance. The phone rings. 'My Mommy's in the shower and can't come to the phone right now,' she tries to say convincingly.

"Cindy is a virtual prisoner for two hours every afternoon until her older brother gets home from high school about 4:30. Her mother arrives about 6:00.

"It's not that Cindy's mother wants it that way . . . not at all. She worries about the tiny girl . . . especially in the area where they live . . . not exactly the best neighborhood. But she was happy to finally find a place that, first of all, she could afford and, second, that would accept children. As to day-care after school . . . that's a luxury the divorcee simply can't afford.

"Cindy is one of a growing number of thousands of latchkey children living in a single-parent family at the borderline poverty level in communities throughout the nation These are tots taught by their parents to fear for their very lives because . . . all too often . . . that's exactly what's at stake . . . unless they take every precaution possible."

## The Theme Approach

An interesting way to provide continuity and help keep the listener's mind "on the track" is by using a central theme or thread throughout the speech. This can be done by weaving a story in and out of the speech, using an appropriate proverb to make each point or telling anecdotes about a certain animal or historical happening.

This "theme approach" was used in this speech for a high school graduation.

". . . The story I'm talking about is *The Wizard of Oz*. It's an intriguing plot—with lots of suspense, action, and colorful characters. It's also an allegory packed with nuggets of truth and wisdom for successful living.

"You will recall that each of the principal characters—Dorothy, the Scarecrow, the Tin Woodman, and the Cowardly Lion—was searching for something. The Scarecrow for a brain; the Woodman, a heart; and the Lion, courage. They were told that the Wizard could give them their heart's desire, so they set off to follow the yellow brick road to take them to the land of Oz.

"Dorothy wanted to go back to Kansas, where everything would be just like it had always been. And she was counting on the yellow brick road to take her there. What Dorothy didn't realize—and we can learn from her—is that we can never go back. The one never-changing certainty of life is that nothing ever stays the same—that everything changes—our relationships, circumstances, people. Nothing will ever be again quite the same as it is this evening.

. . . I hope you have learned to savor each moment as you go—because your yellow brick road is a one-way street, and you can only move forward. Or, as Thomas Wolfe said, 'You can't go home again.'

"As for Dorothy's travelling companions—the Lion, the Tin Woodman, and the Scarecrow—each of them was expecting the

Wizard to solve all of their problems. Certainly others can provide guideposts along the way.

".... What the Lion, the Tin Woodman, and the Scarecrow learned on their trip is a lesson for us all. They found out that the Wizard of Oz couldn't give them their heart's desire. In fact, they found out he was just a phony without any power to help them at all. What they did discover was that the solution to their problem had to come from within themselves ... that they had to make their own pathway on a journey no one else could take for them. They also discovered that they had the personal resources to make their dreams come true.

".... The last thing I think we can learn from the Wizard of Oz is that adversity and obstacles are often very important stepping stones on our journey. The Wicked Witch of the West and even the Wizard himself endangered the security of the yellow brick road travellers. And yet it was through those difficult experiences that they discovered their own inner strength and potential.

"As graduates, it's wonderful to know that you have family, friends, and faculty cheering you on and rooting for you this evening and in the years to come. But, remember! You have to make the journey yourself. Only you can find and travel your yellow brick road."

## THE STATEMENT OF PURPOSE

After you get them hooked on a good, strong opening, you need to tell them what your purpose in your message is. What are they going to get out of listening to what you have to say? This should be stated succinctly and crisply. Here's an example of a statement of purpose.

"This evening we will be discussing the advantages of organizing a neighborhood crime watch group for this area. You will receive a step-by-step plan for starting and running an effective crime watch organization, and I hope, by the time I finish speaking, you will be ready to schedule an organizational meeting."

## THE BODY OF THE SPEECH

This is the meat of the message and should contain three to five main points. No more than three points are preferable. For some reason, people seem to like to think in groups of three. The audience will remember three rules at a time. It's especially effective to use your fingers as a visual gesture as you discuss each point. Numbering the points helps too. Say, "The first thing I would like to say ..." "My second point is ..." "The third thing you need to know about ..."

For example, when using the "gimmick approach" as an introduction technique, as previously mentioned, you would want to elaborate on each one of the three Zs.

1. First of all, your leadership zoom means that it's up to you to zoom out ahead of the group you're leading and to zoom in on your major goals and responsibilities. This means leading by example rather than by clout.

2. Second, use zeal in your dedication and enthusiasm for creating an atmosphere for open communication. This can be broken down to specific ways to do this with employees, with other businesses, and with the public. Use good examples of ways executives have successfully done this.

3. Third, the zest for your leadership position is necessary to build a spirit of unity, a oneness of purpose. That unity has to start at the top, with those who lead. Use case histories and real-life examples of zest and the positive results of leading with zest.

There is also something about listing that seems to motivate people to take notes on what you're saying. Start telling your audience that you're going to give them ten ways to overcome a problem, and watch the pencils and paper come out.

Keep your points simple, couched in everyday terminology. Avoid big words. Speaking in front of an audience is not the place to show off your vocabulary. Avoid using acronyms and technical terms that might possibly be unfamiliar to your audience. If it's a group that has its own language, try to learn one or two of their expressions and throw them in.

Of course, coming up with your three main points can sometimes be a challenge. Initially you may want to write down the following about the topic:

I believe . . .
I think . . .
I feel . . .

Ask yourself, "What are the major units or thought concepts I want to get over to my audience?" After that, come up with the supporting evidence, stories, facts, illustrations—things that will add life to each unit. Also, consider whether an audio-visual aid would enhance and add interest to your presentation.

Check your transitions. Be sure you are not going abruptly from one thought to something completely different. You don't want to leave your listener back at the last thought station while you continue on at 100 miles an hour. Remember that your audience can't go back and reread what you've just said. You have to take them slowly and smoothly to your next point.

Also, you will want to make certain that the anecdotes, quotes, and analogies you use flow directly into the point you are making. This is also true of any audio-visual aids you plan to use. You must be adept at introducing them subtly and easily into the mainstream of your presentation.

## THE CONCLUSION

The conclusion of the speech needs to be very strong and delivered with punch. After all, this is your last shot at them.

State in the final moments what you want your listeners to take away with them. Review what you've said. Summarize the main points you've made.

Using the example of the "three Zs," you might say something like: "Don't forget the three Zs. Zoom out ahead of the group and in on your goals. Show zeal in your enthusiasm for creating an atmosphere for open communication. Be zestful in building a spirit of unity. Practicing the three Zs can take you to a new zenith of excellence and success in the days ahead."

Give your audience a challenge, a plan of action. Show them and give them specific steps they can take to make what you've described a reality.

And then to wrap it all up in a neat package, tie the end back to your introduction.

To put it simply: tell them what you're going to tell them, tell them, and tell them what you told them.

## MAKE IT PERSONAL

Consider: Repetition of fact can be deadly dull for an audience. People are more interested in hearing about people—someone they can relate to—than things.

Statistics can be impressive—up to a point. A recital of numbers soon can result in nodding heads and snoring listeners. Use your imagination to turn your statistics into flesh and bone people. For example, after saying that one in five children lives in a home where the mother is head of the family, talk about a particular family in that situation. Give them names and make them come to life rather than just reciting how much less money the average woman makes than the average man, etc. This approach will keep your audience's interest, and they'll remember little Suzi a lot longer than a bald statistic.

Use personal examples when appropriate. This helps your audience relate to you as a human being and makes you seem more like an old friend. It's amazing how many really good illustrations for speeches occur in our day-to-day lives—once we start looking for them. Keep a small notebook handy to jot down situations as they occur or as you remember them.

Use names of people in the audience to tell a hypothetical (or real) story about. If you don't know the person or if you are a stranger to the group, you will have to rely on the program chairman or others, to give you the name of someone who will enjoy being talked about. This is an excellent rapport builder.

Relate a point to the specific needs and interests of your audience. This may refer to their particular occupation (or types of occupations), their age groups, their community, etc. Or relate a point or story to a specific individual in the audience. For example, "I'm sure Johnny Martin could tell us a lot about body language from his experience as a salesman."

Arrive early enough to get acquainted with some members of the audience and say something like, "I was talking with Kathy Holland before dinner and she said . . ."

Refer to something the group experienced together, e.g., something another speaker has said.

---

## SPEECH ORGANIZATION FORM

Title


What is the purpose of my speech?


How will I open the speech to get my audience's attention?


What is my statement of purpose?


What three to five main points do I want to make?


What examples, anecdotes, humor, statistics, quotes, etc., can I use to support my main points?


How can I summarize briefly what I have said to make my audience remember my main points?


How will I close my speech?

# 7

## Getting Ready
## for the Big Event

### IMPORTANCE OF CAREFUL PREPARATION

Consider: Someone has said that "speeches are like babies—easy to conceive, hard to deliver."[1]

All of us have seen a seasoned, polished speaker and thought how easy it looks. But one thing's for sure, if it looks easy, a lot of hard, tedious work has gone into that presentation before the speaker steps up on the podium.

Plenty of preparation is one of the greatest boons to self-confidence a speaker can have. Lawrence M. Briggs said: "You can't usually tell whether a man is a finished speaker until he sits down."[2] But if when you sit down you want people to think you're a finished speaker beyond being just through, you'll have to pay the price of thorough rehearsal.

Sir Winston Churchill, who moved and inspired men and women around the world with his words, understood the vital necessity of being well prepared and practicing his speeches. Somehow he always managed to find time to rehearse down to the finest detail.

A wonderful story is told about the way he took advantage of every opportunity to practice. It seems that on one occasion, his valet thought he heard him say something through the bathroom door as Churchill was taking a bath. His valet tapped on the door and said, "Excuse me, sir, but were you speaking to me?" "No," Churchill replied, "I was addressing the House of Commons."[3]

One of the most important parts of getting ready for the big occasion is carefully preparing your notes.

## PREPARATION AND USE OF NOTES

Consider: People come to hear a speaker speak, not read. Very few people can read from a script and maintain the audience's interest and attention.

As a rule, a speaker will do a much better job using brief notes written or typed on a few index cards. Of course, this varies with the individual, and you really have to find out what works best for you.

For some speakers a full-blown script serves as a security blanket—in case their minds go blank and they completely forget what to say. Usually they do not plan to use the script in its entirety—only have it handy just in case. As a rule, though, speakers will end up reading a lot more than they had intended to—especially if they become nervous.

Other speakers try to memorize the entire speech—word for word. This can be very dangerous—particularly if there are major distractions during the speech, such as a waiter dropping a tray of dishes or a baby crying.

One of the best approaches that will work well for most speakers is this.

Memorize the opening of your speech and go over it several times. The first few moments are important in developing rapport and you should be free to look at the audience without interruption.

Have your major points and key phrases on 8½ x 5½ index cards. Include direct quotes that you will want to read.

Number your key points. This will help you keep track of where you are.

Use indentation, color coding, and what-have-you to help keep you on track and to remind you to emphasize a point or whatever. Develop your own system—what will work best for you—and stick with it.

Memorize the very end of your speech so that you can conclude with a powerful close, looking directly at your audience.

Of course, there may be an occasion when you will almost have to use a formal word-for-word script, for example, in making a major policy statement address or if the material is of an extremely sensitive nature or has legal ramifications. If so, it is critically important to go over and over and over the script, reading aloud. Try a color highlighter for words or phrases you want to emphasize.

Here are some things to remember in preparing your notes.

• Be sure the writing or type is large enough to see when you are standing at the speaker's stand—even if the light isn't as good as you would like for it to be.

• Use as few cards or pages as possible. The less you have to manipulate, the better off you are.

• Number your cards—just in case you drop them or they get mixed up.

• Use one side only of the cards so you don't have to turn them over. Otherwise, under the pressure of the moment, you may turn the card over . . . and then back over again.

• Don't fold your speech. Chances are it will never be the same as far as resting flatly on the lectern out of view of the audience.

• Don't use a ring binder or a pad. Flipping pages are distracting to the audience.

• Slide pages over as you finish using them rather than stacking them under the unused pages.

• Be sure your stack of pages or cards can safely rest on the speaker's stand without sliding off it if it is made at an angle.

• Hang onto your notes as if they were made of gold. Putting them down and expecting them to stay there can be hazardous to your speaking health.

## HOW LONG IS LONG ENOUGH?

"Let thy speech be short, comprehending much in few words." Ecclesiastes 32:8, The Bible

"To make a speech immortal you don't have to make it everlasting."[4]

An old country preacher used to start his sermons with this prayer:

"Lord, fill my mouth
With worthwhile stuff,
And nudge me when
I've said enough."

"If you would be pungent, be brief: for it is with words as with sunbeams—the more they are condensed, the deeper they burn."[5]

"One of the most important ingredients in a recipe for speech making is plenty of shortening."[6]

"He that thinketh by the inch and talketh by the yard should be kicked by the foot."[7]

Advice to speakers in the words of an old farmer: "When you're through pumping, let go the handle."[8]

"A speaker who does not strike oil in ten minutes should stop boring."[9]

"As I was driving down the road today, I saw two chickens standing there talking. One chicken said she wanted to lay an egg right there in the middle of the road. She asked her friend if she had any suggestions. 'Sure,' said the other chicken. 'Lay it on the line and be quick about it.'"[10]

"Be sincere; be brief; be seated."[11]

"I remember my lesson from the horse and buggy days: The longer the *spoke* the bigger the *tire*."

And Sophocles observed: "To speak much is one thing; to speak well is another."

While all of these sayings are cute and humorous, they make a very serious point. Brevity in speaking is an asset that people appreciate. As a speaker, you don't want your audience to feel like you're holding them prisoners while you drone on and on.

Speaking past the interest point of the listener is kind of like adding water to milk. You'll end up with more liquid, but the quality and taste will suffer. Speaking too long can water down the effectiveness of your message.

It is important to find out from the program chairperson exactly how long he or she wants you to speak. Then observe that time limit religiously. It is considered extremely rude to go over the allotted time since most meetings and programs are carefully planned for a certain time frame. It is also unfair to those who will be appearing on the program later if you wear the audience down to a nub. Speakers who are too long-winded usually aren't invited back.

In all probability, your presentation will last longer when you actually give it than in rehearsal. A good rule of thumb to follow is to allow for about one-fourth more time for the presentation than it takes to rehearse. So if you have been asked to speak twenty minutes, your rehearsal time should run about fifteen to sixteen minutes.

## REHEARSING

Consider: Epictetus, the Stoic philosopher, once said, "No great thing is created suddenly, any more than a bunch of grapes or a fig. If you tell me that you desire a fig, I answer you that there must be time. Let it first blossom, then bear fruit, then ripen."[13]

The old saying "practice makes perfect" may be trite, but it's true.

Going through your entire presentation four to six times is a good way to ensure thorough familiarity and confidence in being able to deliver your material smoothly. There are several ways to rehearse. Ideally, try to simulate as much as possible the actual conditions you will be facing.

After going through the presentation two or three times, use some method of getting feedback. Video taping yourself gives the advantage of being able to see yourself as others see you; it is ideal for honing gestures, facial expressions, enunciation, and other mechanics of speaking. Try to get a friend or member of your family to serve as an audience and give you feedback on clarity, interest maintenance, length, vocabulary, and all those other things that make or break a speaker. In case you don't have access to videotaping equipment and can't con anyone into listening to your rehearsal, practice in front of a mirror to see how you look, and audio tape your voice.

Use something the right height for a speaker's stand. Part of your rehearsal should be manipulating your note cards. One very important thing: if you will be using audio-visual equipment, be sure to practice handling transparencies, changing the pages on a flip chart, or whatever. Otherwise, it's very easy to get bogged down in the mechanics of operating the equipment and forget or foul up what you're saying.

Above all in rehearsing, be aware of the need to sound excited, enthusiastic, and confident of what you're saying.

Winston Churchill believed that the style of the orator is not nearly as important as his sincerity. "Before he can inspire them with any emotion, he must be swayed by it himself. When he would rouse their indignation, he must be swayed by it himself. Before he can move their tears, his own must flow. To convince them he must himself believe. His opinions may change as their impressions fade, but every orator means what he says at the moment he says it. He may be often inconsistent. He is never consciously insincere."[14]

Or, in a lighter vein, every speaker would do well to follow this advice of a veteran circus star to a would-be flying trapeze performer: "Throw your heart over the bars and your body will follow."[15]

# 8

# *Types of Speeches*

Consider: Speaking engagements, like notes at the bank, finally come due.

It would be impossible to even list all the types of occasions and situations a speaker might encounter. However, there are certain kinds of speeches that a speaker is more likely to be asked to give.

The guidelines and samples of some of these types of speeches in this chapter should prove helpful to the person who, out of the blue, is asked to make a certain kind of speech.

## RESPONSIBILITIES OF THE MASTER OF CEREMONIES

Consider: The master of ceremonies is like the minor official at a bullfight whose main function is to open and close the gates to let the bull in and out.[1]

Serving as master of ceremonies is a very important role; in fact the success (or failure) of the whole meeting or event will depend on how well you do your job.

An emcee needs to be not only a good speaker, but also needs to be an attendant to detail. It is important that the emcee arrive early to check out all the arrangements for the meeting and to correct any problems—before the meeting begins.

The master of ceremonies sets the tone for the whole meeting. It's difficult for a speaker to overcome a poor emcee, but a good one will have the audience eager to hear what the

## CHECKLIST FOR THE MASTER OF CEREMONIES

Is the mike (if one is to be used) turned on and working properly?

Does the speaker's stand have a light that works or is it located in a well-lighted area?

Is the room a little too cool for comfort? It will warm up as people start arriving.

Do you know where the thermostat is located and how to adjust the room temperature?

Have you checked the location of wall plugs if A-V equipment is to be used and are extension cords available if needed? Are appropriate stands available? Is equipment in place and operating correctly? Is a screen located for optimum viewing by the audience? Do you have extra projector bulbs ready in case one burns out? Have you made arrangements for someone to turn the lights off and on on cue if this is needed?

Is the room arranged in the best possible way for this particular occasion?

In the case of a dinner meeting, have you made arrangements for tables not to be cleared while the speaker is presenting? This can be extremely distracting and really death for the success of a speech.

Do you have the information needed to make interesting introductions?

If there is to be a head table, do you have the names and titles of those who should be introduced?

speaker has to say.

The emcee must keep the meeting moving and on schedule. A too-long meeting can turn into a tragedy—especially for a banquet speaker who is introduced to give the main address at 10:30 p.m.

The emcee should make sure that the room temperature remains comfortable and have it adjusted if it gets too hot or too cold.

The emcee must be prepared for emergencies.

The emcee should make the people he or she introduces sound interesting and exciting to the audience.

The emcee should not try to be the main attraction—rather a facilitator to keep things on track and running smoothly.

A person who is called on to act as emcee would do well to know the protocol in seating at a formal banquet. Here's the way it goes.

If space permits at the head table, spouses of program participants may also be seated there. But be sure either to seat none of the spouses or all of them. One exception might be the spouse of the honoree if there is not room for the others.

The host or person presiding should be seated at the center of the head table.

To the right of center should be the person being honored, or if there's not an honoree, the main speaker. In case there is an honoree, the featured speaker should be seated to the host's or presider's left with an emcee or toastmaster seated by the main speaker.

Other head table guests should be seated alternately right, left, right, left, according to their rank or importance.

If possible, program participants should be seated at the head table to keep from having unnecessarily long pauses in the program while members of the audience come to the podium.

The program for a banquet would go something like this.

1.  Emcee or person presiding (i.e., club president) makes very brief welcoming remarks including a reference to the occasion.
2.  Emcee introduces person giving invocation.
3.  Invocation is given.
4.  Emcee leads or introduces person to lead the Pledge of Allegiance and national anthem (if used).

5. Dinner, with head table being served first.
6. Emcee thanks the musicians (if there is dinner music) and introduces those seated at the head table (leading in applause after each introduction or asking guests to please hold their applause until everyone has been introduced).
7. Emcee introduces main speaker or introduces person to make introduction.
8. Speaker delivers remarks.
9. Emcee continues applause and thanks speaker and guests, calls for benediction.
10. Benediction.

## SPEECH OF INTRODUCTION

Usually a major task of the emcee will be the introduction of the main speaker, although sometimes an old friend of the speaker will be asked to do the honor. The speech of introduction is very important to the audience and the speaker. It should knit the two together for the time they will spend with each other.

Here are five steps to an effective introduction.

1. Give a preview of the speaker, his or her affiliation, and the topic.
2. Present the speaker's credentials. Why is this particular speaker uniquely qualified to speak on this particular topic?
3. Identify the importance of the subject.
4. Show how the speech will benefit this particular audience.
5. Set an appropriate level of enthusiasm at the conclusion of the introduction by vocal enthusiasm and leading the audience in applause.

These are some important things to keep in mind when you're called on to introduce someone.

The speech of introduction should be brief, not over two or three minutes.

Your role as an introducer is to get the audience ready to listen to the main speaker.

You should tell enough about the person to get the audience interested and to give him or her credibility.

A long recital of a person's life history is tedious and boring. It can put the audience to sleep rather than get them excited about hearing the speaker.

Do give information that will help develop rapport for the speaker. For example, if your speaker is speaking for a Kiwanis Club and is a member of another Kiwanis Club, that information would give the audience an immediate common bond with him.

Don't use the occasion to try to be a comedian or to make a speech on the subject yourself. You may steal some of the speaker's material and leave him or her in an awkward spot.

Do find out what the speaker wants you to tell the audience and use the speaker's introduction if he provides one.

Don't put the speaker on the spot by bragging too much about his or her speaking ability. Don't introduce a speaker as "a silver-tongued orator" or a "speaker without equal." Stick to who the speaker is and what the speaker knows. Let the speaker demonstrate his or her own speaking ability.

The introduction should highlight the person's qualifications for speaking on a certain subject, not bury them in detail. If you are introducing a speaker on a business subject, the fact that the speaker was awarded the Purple Heart when he was in the service a number of years ago would be relatively unimportant. However, if he happened to be speaking for a veterans' group, the audience would be immediately interested in hearing what a Purple Heart holder has to say. The longer a speaker has been out of school the less important it is to tell the audience about degrees. It is better to concentrate on demonstrated performance and recent accomplishments rather than past academic achievements.

As an introducer, you should project an image of the speaker as a competent, interesting person who is abundantly qualified to speak on the chosen subject.

Give the title or subject of the speech—unless the speaker asks you not to.

On occasion you may want to say something to the speaker about the audience in the speech of introduction. For example, you might want to tell the speaker if most of the members had read the speaker's book and requested that he or she be asked to speak.

## SPEECH OF INTRODUCTION OUTLINE FORM

We are fortunate to have as our speaker today

_____, _____
          (full name)

_____ .
      (descriptive phrase about position, accomplishment, etc.)

His/her qualifications and experience in this field include:

_____

_____ .

This topic is important because _____

_____ .

All of us will benefit from hearing what _____

has to say because _____

_____ .

_____ is a native of _____

and a graduate of _____ .

Also, _____
      (information about family, awards, hobbies, etc., if pertinent)

_____

_____ .

_____ 's speech is titled _____ .
      (name)

Please join me in welcoming _____ .
                (speaker's full name)

(Lead applause, shake hands with speaker when it seems natural, and be seated.)

The dignity or informality of your introduction should depend on the occasion, your relationship with the speaker, and the prestige of the speaker.

As a rule, the better known the speaker, the shorter the introduction should be. The president of the United States is always introduced with something like, "Ladies and gentlemen, the President of the United States."

As an introducer, think of yourself holding the speaker by one hand and the audience by your other hand. Then move them together and place each one's hand in the other's. Then move out of the way.

## WRITING YOUR OWN INTRODUCTION

The way the speaker is introduced is critical to the speaker's initial acceptance by the audience. Unfortunately many introducers do the speaker a gross injustice by making him or her sound deadly dull or by trying to steal the spotlight from the speaker. When this happens, the speaker has a real challenge. It may take the first three or four minutes to overcome what the introducer has done to the speaker.

As a speaker, you are taking a big risk when you send an introducer your vita. Have you ever gotten really excited about hearing a speaker once you have sat through a lackluster recital of his birth, every place he went to school, names and ages of children, and on and on ad nauseam? If you are a person of many accomplishments, this reading will probably cut into the time allotted for your remarks besides getting your audience so bored they'll be ready to bolt out the door.

Since this is the case, you might want to seriously consider writing your own introduction and making sure that the person who is going to introduce you receives it. Most introducers will be relieved that they don't have to bother with trying to make up their own, but in case you're concerned that they might be offended, you might title it "background information" rather than "introduction."

Even if you've sent the introducer your introduction in the mail, it's a good idea to take a copy with you to the occasion . . . just in case the original got lost or forgotten. Then check with the person to be sure he or she has it.

Writing your own introduction gives you the opportunity to include only the information about yourself that you believe will be of particular interest to your audience. You also can include past experience and qualifications that lend credibility to your speaking on that specific subject. You can decide whether you want the title of your speech given in the introduction or you may have reason to want to reveal your title yourself, particularly if you plan to use provocative questions to make your audience really wonder what you're leading up to. Another advantage of writing your own introduction is that your opening remarks will, seemingly, spontaneously tie into the introduction.

Having your own introduction ready may save you from the embarrassment of the introducer giving erroneous information, telling weird stories, or turning off your audience before you even have a chance to walk to the speaker's stand.

## THE PERSUASIVE SPEECH

The basic purpose of the speech of persuasion is to sell an idea to the members of an audience, change their minds about an issue, move them to take a certain action, or a combination of these.

The basic appeal of the persuasive speech must be made on psychological grounds. It is important, then, to relate what you have to say to the basic drives and motives of the audience. These include physical well-being, acquisition of material well-being, public approval (desire to be in the "in-crowd"), affection and love of family and friends, and aesthetic tastes.

To be an effective persuasive speaker, you must know as much as possible about the makeup and outlook of your audience. These are some considerations to keep in mind.

What is the average age of the audience? Young people tend to be more liberal and more susceptible to influence, new ideas, and idealistic statements. It takes an energetic, forceful presentation to move them.

What is the existing belief of the majority of audience members? A more logical approach should be used with a hostile group, while a more psychological approach is more effective with an apathetic audience.

Your purpose in addressing apathetic listeners will usually be to move them to take a certain action. With a hostile group, it will be to change opinion.

What is the background and training of the group? The more highly trained listeners are, the more willing they will be to experiment, to try a different approach, a new idea. The audience with less training will require a more forceful presentation. Those with less education respond positively, in general, to an authoritarian approach. However, a speaker who is cocky or extremely dogmatic will turn any audience off.

It is very important to make sure the physical needs and comfort of your audience are met if you expect to move them to do something. A too hot or cold meeting room, a depressing atmosphere, uncomfortable chairs, long meetings without adequate restroom and refreshment breaks will make your job as a persuader extremely difficult.

What is the situation of most of your audience members? If half of your listeners are unemployed or work for a business or industry in the process of making cuts, your chances of inspiring them to get behind the arts in their community are practically nil. You have to meet listeners on the level at which they're functioning. The lower, more basic needs (food, shelter, safety) must be met before higher levels can be addressed successfully.

Here are some tips for choosing material to use in a persuasive speech.

Show your listener what's in it for him or her. Make it personal.

Choose material that's active.

Talk about real things—people, locations, dates—rather than the abstract.

Consider the proximity of the material to the interest and experience of the audience.

Be sure to use examples, case histories, anecdotes that are familiar and of use to the group.

Include material that's novel and unusual.

Use humor, but sparingly and in good taste.

Use persuasive words. A study conducted by Yale University researchers showed that the twelve most persuasive words in the English language are: discovery, easy, guarantee, health, love, money, new, proven, results, safety, save, and you.[2]

## THE INFORMATIVE SPEECH

The purpose of the informative speech is to secure understanding and to assist the listener in learning and evaluating the information presented.

The informative approach is appropriately used in teaching, in training situations, in the presentation of reports, in demonstrations, and in book reviews.

In selecting a topic for the informative speech, keep the following information in mind.

- The nature of the occasion
- Your interest in and convictions about the subject
- Appropriateness to intellectual background and training of the audience
- Suitability for oral presentation
- Goal for this particular audience in relation to the subject

The following strategies are recommended for gathering material.

- Review of previous knowledge on the subject
- Research in reference books, periodicals, books
- Interviews
- Questionnaire

These approaches provide good supportive material for this type of speech.

- Statistical information, rounded off when exactness is unimportant
- Case histories
- Personal examples
- Audio-visual materials
- Use of charts, graphs, and lists
- Handouts
- Vivid and graphic word pictures
- Definitions
- Statements from authorities
- Comparisons and analogies with the familiar

This type of speech is mostly deductive in form, starting with generalities and moving to specific information. Start with the familiar and move to the unfamiliar, using a sequence of ideas. A chronological approach may also be used effectively.

## THE IMPROMPTU SPEECH

Consider: One of the most challenging types of speaking is the impromptu speech, the one you had no idea you were going to be making. Then there you are, suddenly, on your feet before a group of people who are sitting there expectantly waiting for you to say something.

Don't panic. There is a way out without falling flat on your face, and short of dropping dead on the spot.

First of all, don't apologize. Don't say that you had no idea you were going to be called on to say something. Act poised—even if you don't feel poised. Who knows? You may even fool yourself.

Realize that the audience doesn't expect a magnificent speech on the spur of the moment. Most people aren't going to remember what you say anyway.

Act enthusiastic about having the opportunity—even if you don't feel at all thrilled over the turn of events.

Stall for time to get your thoughts together. If the presider asks you to say "a few words" and it's an informal group, you might get up, say slowly, "A few words," and then act like you're going to sit down. Talk about how pleased you are to have been given this opportunity to say something to the group or say something pleasant about the occasion. All the time you're making pleasantries, your brain can be organizing what you're going to say.

Use the "rule of three." There's almost a magical quality about that number for a speaker. It provides mental hooks to hang your thoughts on. You can talk about three things we can do as a group, three things you would like to point out about the occasion or a certain situation, or three things you remember about the person being honored.

Structure your thoughts around the past, present, and future. For example, talk about the tremendous contributions this organization has made in years past, what members are doing today, and how tomorrow promises to be even better.

Use the journalistic approach. Hang your thoughts on the five W's. Talk about who, what, why, when, where (and add how). This, too, gives you a structure—something to help you organize your thinking—quickly.

Speaking off the cuff can be a stimulating, rewarding experience. The most important thing to remember is don't panic. When you have to rise unexpectedly to say a few words, have confidence that you can also rise to the occasion.

## THE ENTERTAINING SPEECH

Although most speakers are not asked very often to give a strictly entertaining speech, there are orators who make a good living specializing in the speech of entertainment. In fact, some of them have just one basic speech they give over and over with only a few changes, such as substituting the names of people in the audience in their stories. Occasionally, however, a speaker will be asked to give a speech with the sole purpose of entertaining the audience.

Banquets and class reunions usually draw the majority of requests for this type of speech. Most after-dinner speakers would do well to make at least the first portion of their speeches entertaining, with some humorous oases worked in from time to time. Otherwise, they may find themselves speaking to after-dinner nappers.

You should consider three main things in preparing an entertaining speech: the makeup of the audience; the occasion; and yourself as a speaker.

Here are some approaches that are effective in developing a humorous speech.

- Make yourself the humorous object of the stories.
- Tell stories on well-known members of the audience.
- Tack an afterthought on the end of an otherwise serious statement.
- Use a surprise ending.
- Exaggerate.
- Make intentional errors.
- Use incongruities.
- Appear to let your tongue slip.
- Pan members of the group.

These are some cautions to keep in mind.

- The entertaining speech should be as carefully prepared and rehearsed as any other speech, perhaps more so.

• Do not use a series of unrelated jokes or stories. Use a theme and transitions to tie anecdotes together.

• The stye of delivery should be intimate—as though you're merely talking with the audience.

• Avoid a sarcastic attitude.

• Remember the old saying, "Brevity is the soul of wit."

• Be sure to speak in an animated manner, using exaggerated facial expressions.

• Last, but not least, don't use any material that might be offensive to any member of your audience.


## THE SPEECH OF WELCOME OR GREETING

The purpose of the speech of welcome is to create a warm, friendly atmosphere for those being welcomed and to set the keynote for the occasion. This type of speech is appropriately given for a number of different occasions: a convention, a conference, a meeting, a special guest or group of visitors, or to welcome new members to a group or organization.

It is a brief presentation—usually no longer than three to five minutes. It should fit the spirit of the occasion. While it usually has some "fluff" and is a little on the flowery side, be sure that you can make your remarks sincerely. A touch of humor is appropriate to get the meeting or occasion off to a pleasant start.

The speech of welcome should contain:

• A reference to the group and occasion

• Complimentary, appreciative statements about the group or person being welcomed or greeted

• Facts about the place or city if participants are from out of town or if the meeting is being held at a historical or significant site

• Expression of expectation and best wishes for a successful, profitable meeting

Here are a couple of examples of the speech of welcome or greeting.

### Welcome to National Association of School Security Directors

It's a special privilege for me to be able to welcome the Texas Chapter of the National Association of School Security Directors. However, I really think your organization is misnamed. I believe I would call it the Association of Problem Solvers. I know of no other people in public education who are constantly called on to rise to so many unusual challenges day in and day out and to solve problems that most people could not even imagine. There are so many problems. It seems like they multiply from day to day. In fact, a lot of folks who used to have problems now have problem areas.

Of course, as is the case with most problems, your problems are people problems. For instance, the young man who didn't kiss his wife for seven years—but then shot a man who did.

Yours is the kind of job that is easily taken for granted. Your work is not readily visible to the general public and, often, even to other school folks. And, of course, much of your contribution is in the form of preventive maintenance.

I want you to know that as a superintendent, I recognize the value and the impact of your contribution as I'm sure your superintendent does. School security makes a significant contribution to the schools. Being very strong on good, sound business practice in the operation of our schools, I would have to say it is one of—if not the most—cost-effective operations in public education today. It pays any good-sized school district to have a security operation . . . and actually saves it money in the long run.

I congratulate you on taking advantage of this opportunity to grow professionally and to get new ideas.

It certainly makes me feel safe to know that we have so many school security directors in our city and school district. We hope your stay with us will be pleasant and productive.

Someone asked me the other day what kind of qualifications you had to have to do our school security director's job. This is what I told him:

"Oh, there's not much to it. You only have to have:
the education of a college president
the executive ability of a financier
the humility of a deacon
the adaptability of a chameleon
the hope of an optimist
the courage of a hero
the wisdom of a serpent
the gentleness of a dove

the patience of Job
the grace of God
and the persistence of the devil."

## Student News Conference

It's a pleasure to welcome you as a group of student journalists to our news conference today. I have been looking forward to this opportunity to meet with you and to interact with newspaper staff members from the various high schools.

As you very well know, writing is a tough taskmaster. I congratulate you on your interest in this area . . . because regardless of what you may do, career-wise, writing well will be a distinct asset to you.

I heard a story about Mark Twain in his early days as a reporter which I thought you might enjoy.

It seems that his editor harped on never stating anything as fact—not even a minute detail—unless he could verify its authenticity from personal knowledge. Well, Twain was sent to cover an important social event. He evidently had learned his lesson well, for this was the story he turned in.

"A woman using the name of Mrs. James Jones, who is reported to be one of the society leaders of the city, is said to have given what purported to be a party yesterday to a number of alleged ladies. The hostess claims to be the wife of a reputed attorney."[3]

Well, another editor's particular pet rule was that names must be obtained in writing all items. He stressed over and over that names are essential. This is the story he got from a cub reporter.

"Last night lightning struck a barn northwest of town belonging to Ike Davis and killed three cows. Their names were Rosie, Isabel and Mabel."

I think this news conference is an excellent idea, and I would like to introduce to you the young lady who organized and made arrangements for it. (Introduction) She has asked that four of us talk a few minutes about some current topics which she feels you will find particularly interesting. She has asked me to discuss the school district's policy on separation of church and state.

Following my discussion, _____ and _____ will talk about grading and reporting. Our final speaker will be _____. He will fill you in on recent legislation relating to student discipline.

I'll be looking forward to seeing the stories that you will be writing as a result of today's news conference. I hope you will remember to send me a copy.

## THE SPEECH OF
## DEDICATION AND COMMEMORATION

The purpose of the speech of dedication or commemoration is to focus on the importance of the occasion and/or those who played a significant role in the event or project.

This type of speech is given for the dedication of a memorial, building, or other area, such as a creative playground, a founder's day, an anniversary, or a historical event.

These types of events are formal occasions so it follows that the language of the speech and the style of delivery should also be rather formal.

The program of dedication or commemoration should contain:

• A brief welcome to the event

• Introduction of special guests, person, or family of person being commemorated or whom structure is being named for

• A statement of the importance of the occasion

• A review of the events leading up to the occasion

• A summary of the use to be made of the building in the case of a dedication

• An acknowledgment of the contribution made by individuals involved, such as architect, builder, etc.

• A challenge to live up to ideals and purpose of organization, past heritage, or whatever

Several brief speeches presenting various viewpoints are usually appropriate on such occasions. For example, the program for a school dedication might go something like this:

Invocation
Pledge of Allegiance
National anthem

Welcome and introduction of special guests . . . School principal

School song

History of school . . . Board president

Purpose of building, expressions of appreciation, comments about person being named for . . . School superintendent

Response . . . Person or family member

Benediction

Reception and tour of building conducted by students

Here are examples of a couple of speeches made at the dedication of a school.

## Welcome for School Dedication

There's an old Spanish dicho or proverb that says: "Mas vale tarde que nunca." "Better late than never."

I know to the members of this community the new _____ Elementary School was a long time in coming. But I'm sure you will agree with me that this beautiful facility was well worth the wait.

In the words of Walt Whitman:

"There was a child went forth every day,

And the first object he looked upon, that object he became.

And that object became part of him for the day or a certain part of the day,

Or for many years of stretching cycles of years.

The early lilacs became part of this child,

And grass, and red and white morning glories, and white and red clover . . .

And all the changes of city and country wherever he went . . .

They became part of that child who went forth every day,

And who now goes, and will always go forth every day."

Certainly this beautiful school will continue to have a major impact on the lives and learning of the students who study here and on the entire community.

## School Dedicatory Remarks

Winston Churchill said: "We mold buildings, and they then mold us."[4]

I couldn't agree more wholeheartedly. I think the surroundings that we provide for our young people have a significant bearing on their motivation for learning and the effectiveness of the job our teachers can do.

Certainly this beautiful building will provide an exciting, inspiring atmosphere for _____ students. I know it has already had a positive effect on student and community morale and spirit.

A leading psychologist says that designs of buildings and even furnishings can definitely affect personality. He offers as a prime example an employment office where new carpeting actually decreased clients' tensions. They immediately and very noticeably became considerably more cooperative and less defensive. The psychologist interpreted their response to be the impact of the pleasant surroundings making them feel positive about themselves—even though they were unemployed.

I am excited to see so many members of the community here today. It tells me that you care very much about the education of your children. Certainly it is impossible for me to overemphasize the importance of that kind of involvement on the part of parents and the total community with the schools.

Your participation in today's event and in school activities throughout the year makes an important statement to your children—that you believe education is important. This beautiful facility also makes a very positive statement—that school is a very nice and wonderful place to be.

This school is beautifully and carefully designed to meet the needs of the individual student. It will mean a great deal to your young people's education and to this entire community.

Someone has said: "Education is a companion which no misfortune can decrease ... no crime destroy ... no enemy alienate ... no despotism enslave. At home, a friend ... abroad, an introduction ... in solitude, a solace ... in society, an ornament. It chastens vice, guides virtue, and gives grace and government to genius. Education may cost financial sacrifice and mental pain, but in both money and life values, it will repay every cost one hundred fold."

As superintendent of the _____ schools, it is my special privilege to dedicate this magnificent new _____ Elementary School to these noble purposes.

## THE COMMENCEMENT SPEECH

The purpose of the commencement speech is to congratulate those graduating for their accomplishment and to inspire them as they go on to greater things.

This is a formal occasion. It follows that the speech should be rather formal in tone, but certainly not stiff or humorless. It should be relatively short, particularly if there is a large group of graduates who have to walk across the stage. Most graduates are too excited to pay attention to long, drawn-out remarks and, realistically, other guests came to see a friend or relative receive a diploma or degree—not to listen to a long-winded speaker. The speaker should address not only the graduates but the other guests as well.

The commencement speech should contain:

• Congratulations to graduates

• Acknowledgment of the importance of the support, contributions, and influence of faculty, families, and friends

• Reference to the future

• Inspirational and motivational thoughts

Here is an example of a graduation speech which a board member made at a high school graduation.

### Commencement Remarks

During the Vietnam War, American prisoners were often confined in what were called tiger cages. Because the Communist guerillas in South Vietnam were constantly on the move through the jungles, they kept their POWs not in fixed prison camps, but in small portable prisons that could be quickly picked up and moved.

That's how the tiger cage was invented. Made from bamboo sticks, the little jails often averaged about five feet in length and approximately four feet in width—obviously too small for most American males to stretch out in.

Year after year, American prisoners of war remained cramped, crowded, and confined in these portable prisons. Can you imagine what that would be like? At least one prisoner lived that way for six long years.

A Navy flier who had experienced this awful type of captivity said: "One night I succeeded in working one bamboo stick loose. That was all I needed to step out, and I was free."

Fortunately, most of us will never have that kind of experience. But how many of us build our own tiger cages and imprison ourselves in a tiger cage of the mind?

Locked within every person's mind are vast possibilities that have never had the chance to be realized. The human mind has tremendous power to dream, to visualize, and to imagine. How tragic that that potentially potent creative power is so often caged in by bars of our own making and rarely allowed to stretch to the fullest degree possible.

This evening I would like to suggest three ways to remove the bamboo sticks from your mind and to release the creative power within you.

1. First of all, remove some words from your vocabulary. As graduates, you've spent twelve years adding to your vocabulary, but I'm here to tell you that there are some words you are better off without. One of those is the word "can't." It's one of the greatest robbers of accomplishment around. Avoid it like the plague.

I used to know a teacher who, at the beginning of the year, would write the word "can't" on the board. She would then take the chalk and with a dramatic sweep cross out the "t" and say: "If you don't learn anything else in my class, I want you to remember that there's only one letter's difference between can't and can. Cross out the 't' and can't becomes can." She would go on to say that she considered can't one of the worst four-letter words around, and heaven help the student who said "I can't" in her class. She drilled that into them until I'm sure, even today, her students feel guilty if they use the word can't.

Another no-no is the word "if." It's so easy to convince ourselves that we could do great things if only . . .

If only I was smarter."

If only I had more money . . . or greater opportunity . . . or a better profile" . . . and on and on.

Gary Gariepy, director of Motivation Associates, says: "The little word 'if' has been the bane of mankind since the days of armed Sparta and cultural Athens. The word itself denotes a condition—and a condition denotes an uncertainty. And uncertainty implies confusion and confusion never leads to success."

"If" focuses our attention on obstacles rather than on assets and positive possibilities.

2. The second bamboo stick remover is setting definite, specific goals.

Of course, just setting goals won't do the job. You can make a beautiful list of things you want to accomplish and sit looking at it and admiring it for the rest of your life.

Think, first, in terms of short-range, achievable goals. Write down specific steps you will have to take to remove them from the paper and make them a reality in your life. Then set a specific date for accomplishing each one of them.

If necessary, enlist the aid of a trusted friend as your official motivator or prodder or nagger—whatever title you want to give—but someone who will help you stay on time and on target in attaining your goals.

Be sure your goals are worthy and big enough to be challenging and exciting. Someone has said: "Aim for the moon, because if you miss, you'll still be there among the stars."

Some years ago a headline told of 300 whales that suddenly died. The whales were pursuing sardines and found themselves marooned in a bog. The tiny fish lured the sea giants to their death. Those huge whales—with vast power—were chasing small, insignificant goals.

A person without goals can come to the end of life only to discover that the bulk of life history can be summarized by:

20 years sleeping

5 years dressing and grooming

3 years waiting on others

1 year talking on the phone

6 years watching television

Without definite, stimulating goals, the routines of life become the ruts of life that lead nowhere.

3. The third bamboo stick remover is to make it up in your mind that you are going to absolutely refuse to fear failure. That kind of fear can be the greatest paralyzer there is—worse, by far, than any stroke.

When you think about it, all of us have failed many times or we wouldn't be here this evening. All of us fell down many times in trying to learn to walk. If you play baseball, certainly you didn't hit a home run the first time you picked up a bat. In fact, heavy hitters—the ones who hit the most home runs—also strike out a lot.

Thomas Edison was once asked how it felt to be a failure after 1200 futile attempts to invent the filament of his great dream, the incandescent light bulb. His response was significant. "I have not failed. I have discovered 1200 materials that won't work."[5]

So often it's what a person does with what happens that spells the difference between failure and success.

Did you know that the honeybee makes her honey from exactly the same nectar with which the hermit spider distills one of the deadliest poisons known?

Julie Andrews is a good example of what I'm talking about. She played the leading lady in the Broadway hit *My Fair Lady*. But when Jack Warner decided to make the play into a movie, he signed up nearly all the Broadway cast with one major exception—Julie. Of course, she was disappointed. But when she was asked to star in *Mary Poppins*, she accepted with relish.

At the Academy Awards, *My Fair Lady* swept the awards with one notable exception. Julie Andrews won the Oscar for her starring role in *Mary Poppins*. In her acceptance speech, she said: "I would like to thank the man who made this possible—Jack Warner."

As you graduate this evening, look to the future with great anticipation and optimism. Don't allow tiger cages to surround your mind and stifle your hopes, your dreams, and your ambitions of what you can be and become.

And now, I would like to congratulate each of you this evening . . . and your families and teachers . . . on the goal you have reached. It is an important goal—one which has required a great deal of effort and self-discipline. It is a landmark accomplishment in your lives—one in which you can take justifiable pride.

As the official representative of the Board of Education of _____, it is my pleasure to present the diplomas to the _____ graduating class of _____ High School. On behalf of the entire board and all officials of the _____ schools, I extend my very best wishes for your future success.

## THE SPEECH OF TRIBUTE OR AWARD

The purpose of the speech of tribute or award is to acknowledge and honor a person, persons, or group for outstanding accomplishment, service, or dedication.

This type of speech is appropriately given for the following occasions: presentation of a prize, plaque, or other award in a contest; retirement or going-away party for an employee leaving a firm; outgoing officer of a club or other organization; banquet honoring a person for outstanding service to the community; recognition of a person performing a heroic or noble deed.

The person presenting the award should be familiar with the recipient or at least know enough about the person to make his or her remarks warm and personal. A touch of humor may be appropriate, depending on the particular situation. Cautions include: don't let the occasion become too sweet and syrupy to the point of embarrassing the honoree, and don't exaggerate the accomplishment or deed out of all proportion. In the case of a retirement, be sure to emphasize the happy side.

The speech of tribute or award should contain:

- Very brief welcome to occasion
- Pertinent information about the award or occasion
- Accomplishments and virtues of the person being honored
- Presentation

Here is an example of a speech of tribute given at an appreciation dinner for a community leader who was moving to another city.

### Speech of Tribute

The Good Book tells us that there is a time for all things, a time for every purpose under the heavens—a time to keep silence and a time to speak. And I am glad that today the time has come to speak about the many contributions that _____ has made to the _____ school district, the boys and girls who attend our schools, and the citizens of this community.

Speaking of time, _____ reminds me of a good watch—open faced, pure gold, quietly busy, and full of good works.

Open faced, he is a man of commitment—to his church, his community, to public education and to his personal convictions. I have been impressed with his integrity in standing up for what he believes in—whether it's the popular stance or not.

Pure gold, he has provided stalwart leadership for the _____ schools as president of the school board for the past three years and as a member for the past six years. He has provided the leadership to bring the schools through a time of great pressures and problems. Through this positive guidance, he turned what could have been crisis times into times of fertile opportunity. He has brought distinguished credit to the _____ schools as he has represented us on the state and national levels.

Quietly busy, he is unassuming and humble about his many significant contributions. He stays current and well-informed on all matters pertaining to the _____ schools —no small attainment in a school district of this size and scope. During the brief time I have had the privilege of working with him, I have been extremely impressed with his knowledge and grasp of the problems and challenges facing urban education.

Full of good works, he gives unstintingly of not only his time but of himself. He devotes what would be a full working week for most people to the _____ schools without any remuneration and certainly at the expense of his business and time with his family.

The _____ schools and the people of this community owe _____ an overwhelming debt which mere words cannot convey. He has been a real force for stability, for improvement, for positive change. His influence and contributions will be sorely missed by all in this community.

There is a time for all things. And since he feels that it is time for him to move on to other challenges, I am glad to have this time tonight to pay tribute to an outstanding person and an effective leader.

God bless you, _____.

## THE ROAST

The roast has become an increasingly popular way to pay tribute to a person of accomplishment and service in a lighthearted, fun-filled, tongue-in-cheek manner. While a well-done roast is fun for everyone, it is probably one of the most difficult types of speeches to write . . . and to give, especially for the person not blessed with a flair for comedy.

A whole evening, complete with a dinner, is usually devoted to the roast. Since there are always several people invited to roast the honoree, remarks should be kept short.

Some tips to use in roasting the honored one are:
• Use exaggeration
• Pick on a prominent physical feature or ingrained habit (but be sure it's not one the roastee is sensitive about)
• Tell a humorous incident about the honoree that really happened
• Tell a proven joke and make the roastee the central figure
• Make up some ludicrous, obviously untrue tale and tell it as though it actually happened
• Eliminate any material that might offend or embarrass the honoree or anyone in the audience
• Make it broad enough to be obviously untrue but true enough to fit the roastee's personality and manner of operating

Here is an example of a roast speech given for a baldheaded civic leader.

### Roast

I have really been looking forward to this occasion with relish. After being the roastee at the hands of _____ recently, it's good to be on the other end of the fire this time.

The only problem is that _____ has so many shining attributes, it's hard to find a flaw to focus on like you usually do when you're roasting someone. (pause) But then, of course, if you stop to think of it, one of his attributes is shinier than all the others.

In fact, it got him into a lot of trouble when he was city attorney. I guess it was pretty embarrassing being in that kind of position and getting arrested. You see there were all these wrecks on the Central Expressway. The Police Department was completely overwhelmed with calls. Traffic was tied up for blocks. No one could decide what was causing all the accidents. Finally they figured it out.

_____ was driving down Central at noon in a convertible, and the glare from his head was blinding all the motorists. He was arrested for being a public menace.

He entered a contest once . . . claimed he had more hair on his head than a cue ball. (Pause) The cue ball won.

But one thing I can say about _____, he's not at all sensitive about his lack of hair. He says instead of thinking of himself as bald, he thinks of other people as hairy.

You know I don't think many people really realize the lasting contribution _____ made to the City of _____. He worked tirelessly to get some really important laws on the books. As a result of his dedicated efforts, we are now blessed with some outstanding ordinances that few cities can boast of.

For example, he put a stop to all those convict-types who were feeding pigeons in downtown _____.

Thanks to _____, the city jail is full of criminals who could not resist the urge to climb a tree in a city park.

He also made it illegal for lawless citizens to ride a bike with no hands.

He put an end to citizens herding their cattle across a public street.

Now that's what I call a real contribution.

You know _____ is an outstanding lawyer, but like every counselor at law, it took him a while to get his practice cranked up and going strong.

When he first got out of law school, he opened his law office and sat there expectantly, waiting for his first client. Finally, this man walks in and _____ didn't want him to know how inexperienced he was. So he grabbed the phone and said: "No, I'm very sorry, but I can't take your case, not even for $1,000. I'm just too busy."

He hung up the phone and looked at his caller. "And now, sir, what can I do for you ?" he asked briskly.

The man said, "Oh, nothing really. I just came to connect your telephone."

You may not know it, but _____ is quite an athlete. He's really an ace at tennis. Why, he even beat _____ in a big match. Of course, she had sprained both her wrists and was holding the tennis racket in her teeth . . . but he won.

I'll tell you one thing, though, I have really learned a lot from _____. I've studied his administrative style as executive director of _____. It's amazing the way he operates. I'd never seen anything like it ... couldn't quite find the right words to describe it. But finally I realized that as an administrator, _____ is like an iceberg—ten percent visible, ninety percent submerged, and a hundred percent at sea.

# 9

# *Conducting Meetings*

## ARRANGEMENTS FOR MEETINGS

Consider: Meetings, like certain forms of wildlife, are protected under the law. The First Amendment to the Constitution of the United States says in part that "Congress shall make no law . . . abridging . . . the right of the people peaceably to assemble." Under this guarantee, meetings seem to have multiplied like rabbits . . . until today it seems that everyone is on his way to or from a meeting.

Remember this simple definition of a meeting: "A meeting is a group of people who have come together for a common purpose." Of course, the challenge is seeing that the purpose is accomplished.

One aspect that has a greater impact on the success of a meeting than most people might imagine is the meeting room itself and the way it's arranged.

These are some considerations.

• Lighting should be bright enough for people to write but not so bright that there's a glare. Can the lighting level be controlled?

• Acoustics should be such that speakers can be easily heard all over the room. Carpet helps acoustics. It also is easier on the feet for a presenter or chairperson who will be standing most of the meeting. It is better not to use microphones unless absolutely necessary. They tend to inhibit some people and can

Here are some good arrangements for meetings.

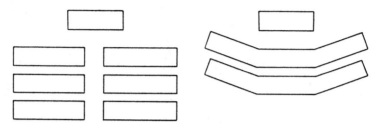

These arrangements encourage good group interaction.

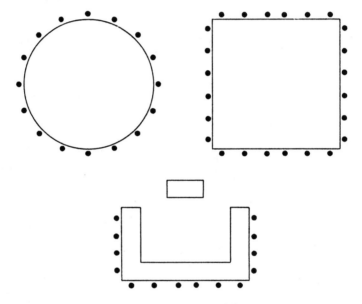

(about twenty maximum)

And this arrangement facilitates small groups within a group interaction.

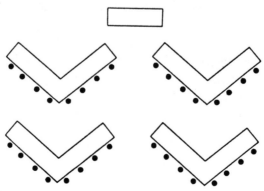

slow down a meeting if a person has to change location in order to speak.

- Are heating and cooling adequate and reliable?
- Are there enough electrical outlets conveniently located?
- Are adequate speaker's stands, tables, etc., available?
- Chalkboards on a stand, rather than an easel, are sturdier. Black is better than green for visibility.
- A room without windows provides for less distraction.
- Posts should not obstruct vision.
- Select the proper room size. Allow about 800 square feet for thirty people with tables and chairs, about 1,000 square feet for fifty people.

## SEATING ARRANGEMENTS

One of the most important things to consider is how to arrange seating for a particular type of meeting. The closer the participants are to the presenter or presider, the better. It is also easier to generate interaction, enthusiasm, cohesiveness, motivation, and team spirit when members of the group are seated close together. For this reason, it is a good idea to use narrow tables.

A good rule of thumb is to set up for about ten percent fewer people than you actually expect to come. It's always better to add more chairs than to have too many empty seats.

## CONDUCTING EFFECTIVE BUSINESS MEETINGS

Consider: Business meetings can be expensive to your organization in terms of man-hours and can turn into endless bores that accomplish little unless they are well planned and run.

The following are some suggestions for keeping a meeting on time and on target.

PRIOR TO CALLING A MEETING:

1.  Ask yourself, "Is this meeting really necessary?" Consider other possibilities.
    Try a conference call to see if an agreement can be reached by phone.
    Write a memo outlining the issue and asking for a

## CHECKLIST FOR PLANNING MEETINGS

### Prior to the meeting
**Publicity:**
___Notices
___Letter of invitation
___Bulletin boards
___Personal contacts
___News release (if appropriate)

**Agenda:**
___Plan agenda
___Plan for involvement
___Contact people on agenda
___Previous minutes
___Committee reports
___Materials needed

**Space and Equipment:**
___Place reserved
___Equipment reserved

### Just before the meeting
**Space:**
___Room arrangement
___Seating arrangement
___Extra chairs
___Climate control

**Equipment and Supplies:**
___A-V equipment set up, checked
___Extension cords
___Microphones

___Gavel, felt pens, pencils, pads
___Newsprint
___Visual aids
___Agenda, other handouts
___Name tags

### At the meeting
___Meeting, greeting, seating participants and guests
___Greeting and seating latecomers
___Handing out materials
___Operation of equipment
___Recording meeting

### End of meeting . . . and after
___Collect unused materials
___Return equipment
___Clean up
___Thank helpers
___Read and analyze evaluation, feedback
___Remind people of follow-up commitments
___Make plans for next meeting, date, etc.
___Send copy of minutes to participants

response to a proposed solution by a certain date. Try to consolidate discussion with an already scheduled meeting.

2. Keep the meeting as small as possible by inviting only those who will be making the decision.
3. Clearly define the purpose of the meeting and let participants know in advance exactly what is to be accomplished.
4. Send out an agenda in advance with the most important item at the top.
5. Set a time limit for the entire meeting and for each agenda item.
6. Schedule the meeting before lunch, another meeting, or an engagement to help ensure that the meeting will end on time.
7. Select an appropriate room for the size and makeup of the group.
8. See that the room is arranged for optimum interaction. The closer the group sits to one another, the easier it is to generate enthusiasm, cohesiveness, and motivation.
9. Consider several alternative solutions prior to the meeting and develop backup information, costs, possible outcomes for each possibility.
10. Figure up how much this meeting will cost the company in salaries, etc., per hour.

DURING THE MEETING:

1. Start on time regardless of who is missing.
2. Assign someone to take notes and keep time on each agenda item.
3. Clearly define the purpose of the meeting.
4. Stick with the agenda.
5. Limit interruptions to emergencies.
6. Restate conclusions for clear understanding and to ensure a commitment of purpose.
7. Make assignments with due dates clearly stated.
8. End on time.

---

## MEETING EVALUATION FORM

(Please check the appropriate answer.)

___yes___no  Did you feel this meeting was necessary?

___yes___no  Was the purpose of the meeting clearly defined?

___yes___no  Did you receive a copy of the agenda before the meeting?

___yes___no  Did you receive backup materials to study in advance?

___yes___no  Was adequate attention given to answering questions?

___yes___no  Did the meeting start on time?

___yes___no  Was the agenda followed?

___yes___no  Was the purpose of the meeting accomplished?

___yes___no  Were conclusions summarized accurately?

___yes___no  Were assignments made clearly?

___yes___no  Were realistic time frames set for completion of assignments?

___yes___no  Was the meeting room suitable and appropriately arranged?

What suggestions would you make to improve future meetings?

---

AFTER THE MEETING:

1. Send notes of meeting, listing assignments and due dates, to participants and any other staff members affected by the decisions.
2. Follow up with progress reports on implementation of decisions.
3. Have each participant turn in an evaluation of the meeting.

## BRAINSTORMING

Consider: Brainstorming is probably the best technique available to get a group of people communicating and working effectively together. It breaks down barriers in rank and often results in some excellent, workable strategies for solving a problem or for implementing a new thrust or program.

The purpose of brainstorming is to obtain as many ideas as possible in a given time period. Quantity is welcomed. No idea is to be discussed or judged. It is absolutely forbidden for anyone to grimace, make a negative comment, or put down another's idea.

Appoint someone in the group to record the ideas. Have the recorder write them with a felt pen on big sheets of newsprint or on a chalkboard so all group members may see them.

### Instructions to Facilitator

Briefly explain the topic, problem, or goal for the brainstorming session. Go over the ground rules for brainstorming at the top of this page.

Limit the size of the group to about seven or eight participants. In a larger group, divide into smaller groups for brainstorming.

Give participants two or three minutes to ponder the subject and think of several ideas.

Go around the table and have one participant at a time state an idea in a short, complete sentence.

Make sure all ideas are recorded.

Don't allow any criticism or discussion of any idea.

Canvass the group as many times as needed to encourage participants to express all their ideas. Participants may pass when they run out of ideas.

Arrange for the ideas to be typed in a list or written on a smaller piece of paper if they're to be the object of additional discussions later in the same session.

Arrange for any ideas participants may have after the session to be added to the list. Often participants will get their best ideas after a session is over.

### Ranking

When participants have the complete lists at hand, ask each member to rank the five they feel are the best from one for the top down through five. This may also be done by a show of hands when the ideas are still on the newsprint or chalkboard.

Compile the individual rankings to derive the group ranking of the best ideas.

Discuss the best ideas for reaching the stated goal or solving a certain problem.

One may be selected as the very best and a plan of action developed from it.

If more than one small group has brainstormed, get the whole group back together and have a member of each group report on what they came up with.

Or you can have individual groups brainstorm different aspects of a question, develop a plan, and then report back. An example might be communicating with employees, with one group taking effective ways to communicate with office personnel, another with maintenance and custodial workers, and a third with professional employees.

### Advantages

Since all ideas are welcomed, regardless of merit, all members feel they may participate as equals.

A great number of ideas can surface in a short time, and some are sure to be worth considering.

There is no time-wasting discussion of the merits of all ideas.

Participants will start to bounce off of each other with one's ideas sparking a new idea in someone else.

It is an excellent vehicle to develop rapport among members of a group and a great way to get acquainted.

## HANDLING TYPES OF PARTICIPANTS
## IN MEETINGS

Consider: Basically you will find two groups of participants in meetings: those who are eager to talk and those who don't want to talk at all. Trying to involve the non-talkers and to keep the talkative ones from dominating a discussion is a real art, requiring great diplomacy and skill. As a presider, it is important and to your advantage to remain cool and collected at all times and to always give dignity to the participants—even if they are being rude and contentious.

| **Type of Participants** | **Solution** |
| --- | --- |
| Ax grinders | Discuss the situation if it fits the subject under discussion. Otherwise, indicate an interest in the person's problem and offer to discuss it after the meeting. |
| Non-stop talkers | Interrupt when they take a breath and summarize what's been said. Then ask someone else a question. If they persist, say something like, "Jim might have some insight into this particular question." |
| Blase Brendas and aloof Als | Try to tie the discussion into their area of expertise or experience. Ask them to share their wisdom. |
| Racial or political expounders | State that those particular issues cannot be discussed in this meeting. |
| Whisperers | Stop talking and look at individuals. Ask one of them a ques- |

tion or an opinion.

Illogical concluders

Say something like, "That's an interesting perspective."

Stubborn standers

Recognize that they may not really understand the issue under discussion or the ramifications. Get them to expand on their point of disagreement. Restate your premise. Get others to help you explain. Or, as a last resort, offer to discuss the question with them later.

| **Participant's Behavior** | **Solution** |
| --- | --- |
| Contentious spirits | Try to ignore their comments by pretending not to hear them. Recognize any legitimate complaints. Offer to discuss it with them after the meeting. Assign someone who has responsibility in the area of their complaint to talk with them privately about the problem or concern. Often the group will help you take care of an obvious troublemaker. As a last resort, take them aside and try to enlist their cooperation. |
| Silent Sams and Samanthas | Ask them a direct, provocative question. |
| Participants arguing among themselves | Interrupt with a direct question. Bring other audience members into the discussion. Ask that the discussion be limited to the facts. |
| Strayers from the subject | Comment, "Someday perhaps we can talk about that, but right now we need to finish our discussion on _____." |

| | |
|---|---|
| Poor speakers | Recognize that they may have great ideas but are limited by fear or vocabulary. Restate their contribution by saying something like, "In other words, you think . . ." |
| Radicals | Say, "Well, of course, you're entitled to your opinion." |
| Eager answerers | The person who always wants to answer first can easily sabotage your efforts to involve as many as possible in the discussion, especially if they blurt out the answer without being recognized. A good way to handle this person is to say, "After our discussion of this question, I'm going to ask _____ to summarize what's been said." |
| Shrinking violets | Ask direct questions you are sure they can answer. Ask if they agree with a statement. Comment favorably if they do get the courage to contribute. |
| Ramblers | When they come up for breath, thank them, rephrase one of their statements, and call on someone else or go on to the next topic. |

## GUARANTEED SNAFUS FOR MEETINGS

*Keep members waiting.* As chairperson, arrive on time . . . and *then* start getting ready for the meeting. Next meeting more members will arrive late, assuming that the meeting will not begin on time anyway.

*Do all the planning yourself.* People will support what they feel they have a part in planning and carrying out. Ask others for suggestions, advice on how to improve future meetings, or let a committee assist with the planning.

*Conduct every meeting exactly the same way—without variation.* While some people cling to routine, most people find it monotonous over a long period of time. Add a little festivity occasionally by moving to a more glamorous setting or by serving some really interesting refreshments.

*Fail to plan for the best arrangement of the room.* A classroom style seating arrangement is not conducive to group discussion. Decide in advance what will work most effectively for this particular meeting.

*Don't make sure equipment is working and audio-visual material can be seen and heard.* Probably nothing is more irritating to an audience than mechanical failures and illegible or inaudible media approaches.

*Assume that everyone knows the purpose of the meeting.* The goal or goals of the meeting should be stated when the meeting is called and at the beginning of the meeting.

*Don't have a prepared agenda.* Discussing whatever comes up is a sure way to lose the interest and support of the very people who are the most important to your success. A prepared agenda helps keep the meeting on track and gives you something to point to when members stray from the subject.

*Let a few people hog the meeting.* Some of your best insights and suggestions may come from members who are not aggressive enough to shout down incessant talkers. It's up to the chairperson to ensure that each person present has an opportunity to contribute.

*Neglect having notes taken of the meeting.* A summary of the meeting is important for future reference and in making sure that assigned tasks are being carried out by their due dates. A copy of the minutes should be sent to all those present, members who were unable to attend, and others affected by the decisions or plans.

*Don't have a definite time to end the meeting.* Most people are simply too busy to attend meetings that drone on and on. They want to know how long the meeting is scheduled to last and that they definitely will be through at that time.

# 10

# *So You're Going to Be on Television*

Consider: Appearing on television is definitely a different type of experience from speaking in front of an audience. Few people have the opportunity to become acquainted with this unique environment before actually being thrown into it.

The following tips may be useful if you suddenly find you're going to be an interviewee on a television program.

## WHAT TO WEAR

• As a rule, television will make people look several pounds heavier than they actually are. An outfit that is slenderizing can be a real plus. Solid colors for major items of clothing such as a suit or dress are safest. Big, bold patterns are distracting and call attention away from the interviewee. It's better to shy away from bright white. Pastel colors are safer for, say, a man's shirt. Avoid wearing fabrics of high sheen. Lightweight clothing will be much more comfortable under the bright lights.

• Shiny jewelry should be avoided as should any jewelry which might make a noise, such as a charm bracelet. A necklace or tie clasp could also cause problems by hitting a lavaliere microphone or the microphone cord.

• Men should wear socks that cover the calf. This eliminates the possibility of an ankle shining forth if legs are crossed. Also, socks should match the pants. Remove items such as wallets, glasses, and keys from your pockets.

• Consider how your outfit will look when you're seated. For example, a short, tight skirt on a woman can be a disaster on screen.

• Simplicity is an excellent rule to follow.

## HOW TO PREPARE

Watch the show you'll be appearing on several times if possible. This will give you a feel for the format, the type of questions the host usually asks, and the overall tone of the show.

If you're not accustomed to bright lights, consider talking at home with the brightest lights you can find shining in your eyes.

If you're going to be interviewed, get a friend or relative to practice with you as the interviewer until you become thoroughly at ease with that format and sound conversational.

If you need statistics or direct quotes, print or type these on individual index cards.

If you have any kind of visual material you would like to use, check it out with the program host well in advance of the program. As a rule, it's better to have the material or object set up somewhere in the studio rather than your trying to hold it steady on camera.

Arrive early for the interview. This gives you the opportunity to become familiar with your surroundings and perhaps the chance to discuss your interview in greater depth with the program's host.

## DURING THE PRODUCTION

Be sure to make clothing adjustments as needed before the session begins. Men will usually need to pull coats down in back because they hike up on the neck when seated.

Always look at the person you're talking to. Make eye contact with the person interviewing you. If it's a group discussion and someone else is speaking, give that person your undivided attention.

If you want specifically to address the viewer, for example, if your host gives you the opportunity to make a direct appeal for funds in a charity drive you're representing, look directly into the camera.

Try to be as natural and conversational in tone as possible.

Keep your shoulders parallel to the floor and your head up straight. Otherwise, you'll appear to be a listing vessel.

While gestures are fine, be on guard against sudden, darting movements. Pity the poor director who has a tight closeup of your face and it suddenly disappears from view.

Be sure not to touch the the microphone or its cord.

Time cues will be agreed upon before the show begins. While time is the responsibility of the production staff and your host rather than yours as a guest, you need to be sure not to get into a long, involved explanation when there's only a minute left in your segment of the show.

If you don't understand the question, don't hesitate to ask for clarification.

If an untrue statement is made, refute it diplomatically.

If you are asked a series of questions, pick the one you want to answer most and give that information first.

## SOME CAUTIONS

Unless you're accustomed to using a teleprompter (in the case of some type of prepared statement or use of quoted material), don't attempt it. Using a teleprompter smoothly takes a lot of practice and can be disastrous when done awkwardly.

Once the program begins, assume your microphone is on at all times. If you don't want something on the air, don't say it.

Never look off the set, regardless of what happens. Resist the temptation to be distracted by what the crew is doing. Concentrate completely on the interview.

A special warning should be heeded about looking at the studio monitor. There have been occasions when guests have gotten so fascinated by watching themselves on the monitor that they completely lost contact with what was happening in the interview.

Be sure to keep your language simple, especially if you're talking about a technical subject. Assume that your listener knows little or nothing about your field.

Don't get bogged down in a string of statistics or a long, drawn-out explanation. You'll lose your viewer.

Always remain seated until you are told you may leave the set. Watch those chairs! If you're seated in a swivel chair, don't swivel. One with rollers can be disastrous, especially if you're seated on a platform.

Don't ever assume you're off camera, even when others are speaking. The director may decide to come to you for a reaction shot at the very moment you decide to scratch your nose.

## THE REPORTER COMETH

Consider: Certainly one of the most unusual speaking situations you can find yourself in is the television news story interview. Unless you are a public figure, you probably won't have this experience more than once or twice in a lifetime. But just in case this happens to you, take some tips from Dean Angel, former television news reporter.

QUESTION: Dean, what advice would you give a person who is called for an interview by a television reporter?

DEAN: Determine why the reporter is calling in the first place. Find out if it's strictly for information or if there's an underlying motive. I also would caution the interviewee not to necessarily answer a question the way it's raised. Usually a reporter phrases a question for a specific reason or to lead to something else.

QUESTION: You might say more than you wanted to?

DEAN: Yes, that's quite likely. You want to be sure to present your answer in a way that gives only the information you want the reporter to have. The reporter's underlying motive for talking with you is what you want to find out. Often reporters will ask questions that aren't really related to the story—just chit chat to make the subject comfortable. Then, suddenly, they'll spring a leading question. As an interviewee, you're much better off if you can stay in control of the interview rather than being defensive and giving the reporter free rein.

QUESTION: How would you describe the job of a reporter?

DEAN: Well, you have to remember that a reporter is employed to produce news stores. His job is to sell stories, not just pass along information. He doesn't spend his time just giving information about a meeting that the group desires. He has to get gutsier. It's the story the reporter goes out and gets (as opposed to one like the opening of a new museum) that you have to be careful of.

So many people you go to interview say, "We don't want any publicity on this." Well, of course, it's not the business of the reporter to give publicity, but to deliver a story viewers or readers will find appealing, interesting, or controversial. It's also not his business to conceal what you don't want known.

QUESTION: What makes a news story?

DEAN: The unusual, the unique. The first is always a key. Someone does something for the first time, that's news. It's not news the second time—even though someone else does the same thing bigger, better, and more beautiful.

Controversy is also news. Usually the reporter will bring out both sides. The viewer can identify with one side or the other and thereby becomes a part of the story.

A disaster or tragedy is also news, automatically bringing the casual bystander into the reporting arena.

QUESTION: What suggestions would you give someone who suddenly becomes a central figure in a controversial situation?

DEAN: Well, of course, that covers a variety of circumstances. As a general rule, though, it's better to be open and up front, that is, if you don't have anything to hide. The worst thing you can do is say "no comment" or "talk to my attorney," especially if you're already on camera. Some people who are frequent interviewees have found that being "unavailable for comment" is a better line.

But if you act evasive, the reporter may decide there's more to it and keep on digging. And if you're open, it may die for lack of controversy or it may be only a one-time story. Once you're on television, you become like an acquaintance to the viewer. Someone with a good personality who can project well oftimes can override the issue. Remember, too, whoever gets to tell his side of the story first has an advantage.

QUESTION: What about giving "off the record" comments?

DEAN: It's safer not to make "off the record" comments

unless it's something you really want the reporter to know. You can't count on it not becoming a part of the story. In fact, I think a lot of reporters interpret "off the record" to mean, "Don't quote me, but here's the information. Now, that you know the information, get it from another source."

QUESTION: What's the length of the usual television news story?

DEAN: Around a minute. The reporter's job calls for briefness. Reporters have to be gifted in keeping it short. If you're being interviewed, it's important to be concise and not go into minute detail. Extraneous material can hurt you. The reporter may interview you for fifteen minutes and use only ten seconds of the interview. And he may cut out facts that you want included. You must realize that while you may have all the facts to prove your case or position, the questions may never allow you the opportunity to give them. Once you get into the interview situation, the reporter may start nipping at you in a manner very foreign to his/her original "Mary Sunshine" demeanor.

QUESTION: It sounds dangerous.

DEAN: Well, it can have its hazards. You really can't afford to be naive. On the other hand, though, I want to emphasize that being shown in a bad light on the ten o'clock news isn't the end of the world. Chances are that thirty-second clip will be the only thing that's ever said. In a major market, the viewership is split between several stations and once it's been aired, it's gone. It's not like a newspaper story that can be passed around, thumbtacked to the bulletin board, and kept on microfilm forever.

QUESTION: What if a reporter makes an error?

DEAN: Television station news organizations don't make corrections—except occasionally within the same telecast. It's really impossible to make corrections because you never have the same viewers for any two news reports.

QUESTION: Could you give some specific tips for the interviewee during the actual interview?

DEAN: Yes. These are some things to remember.

Be conversational in tone, using simple, everyday language.

Interesting facial expressions and spontaneity are definite assets.

Always look at the person asking the question, not at the

camera.

A nice touch is to call the reporter by name, especially if it's an important point you don't want to end up on the cutting room floor. It gets his name on once more and it gives the impression he's well-known. He'll like that line when it comes to editing.

Remember that the reporter wants to show feeling not just facts. Descriptive phrases are good.

Get to the point quickly. Don't ramble.

QUESTION: Do you have any other suggestions?

DEAN: I would suggest occasionally watching television news reports with a stop watch and note pad. Analyze the program. How many seconds is an interviewee actually on camera during a story? What types of comments and material does the reporter actually use? Was the question used or part of an answer? Could it have been out of context? Did it appear to be a fair representation of facts? Learning to control the interview and be a good interviewee takes practice. The average person doesn't have the opportunity to practice. But a person who anticipates being thrust into that role might consider the possibility of doing simulated interviews with a friend asking probing, relentless questions. There are some seminars around that use this technique.

I certainly don't intend to put reporters in a bad light. Indeed, most are doing their job well and it's a difficult task.

The nature of reporting for a commercial organization means that reporters who make themselves stand above others get the promotions and the salaries. So, there's an eagerness to make every story appealing for the audience, the news director, and the assignments editor. Blended with this compelling effort is the journalist's creed to be honest, fair, and truthful, and to continue to warrant the U.S. Constitution's First Amendment right of speech and press freedom. At the intersection of these two forces lies the reporter—and it's a difficult position to hold.

# 11

# *Getting Organized as a Speaker*

## SETTING GOALS AS A SPEAKER

Consider: Becoming an effective public speaker doesn't just happen overnight. It takes effort, experience, and action.

Once you've made the decision to become the best public speaker you can possibly be, you can turn that desire into a reality a lot quicker by setting some definite goals. The following steps for setting and attaining goals are good ones to take to help you reach your destination. Even if you're a good speaker, this process can help you to become even better.

1.  Write down the goals you want to reach in speaking, making them as specific as possible. Don't just say "to be an excellent speaker." List the areas in which you need to improve.
2.  Rank goals in priority order. Which one is most important to reaching your overall goal?
3.  Write down obstacles to reaching each goal and develop a concise, step-by-step plan for overcoming each one.
4.  Develop a time frame for reaching each step for your goal.
5.  Picture yourself positively completing each goal.
6.  Make yourself accountable to someone else (if that's what it takes) for completing each step on time. It's

great if you have a friend who is also working toward improving speaking skills and you can make a pact to monitor, encourage, and critique one another.

Let's take an example.

Say you decide that you need a greater vocal range, better breath control, and more self-confidence.

You decide on these priorities.

• More self-confidence
• Better breath control
• Greater vocal range

In analyzing the situation, you determine that you're never going to gain more confidence without a lot of practice before an audience. Your plan might include the following.

• Speak at every opportunity.
• Make your own opportunities by volunteering to give a report, or running for a club office that entails speaking, such as program chairperson.
• Join Toastmasters International.

Your plan for developing better breath control might look something like this.

• Set aside a minimum of ten minutes each day to practice breathing exercises. (Some are listed in Chapter 3.)
• Improve overall physical condition by exercising at least three times each week.
• Purchase a tape recorder and read a certain passage once a week.

Compare the breath support and endurance with your previous week's reading.

Your steps to developing a wider vocal range could include the following.

• Set aside at least ten minutes a day to do exercises. (Some are included in this book.)
• Use the tape recorder to read a passage, and a piano or pitch pipe to determine your speaking range.
• Record the same passage each week and compare the range with the previous week's effort.

Your time frame might be to increase your speaking range by at least one note in a month's time.

## FINDING MATERIAL

Where can you find good material to use as a speaker? The answer is just about anywhere . . . and everywhere. Once you become attuned to seeing good illustrations and anecdotes in your everyday life, you'll be amazed at what you'll come up with.

Always carry a notepad with you to jot down incidents you observe, hear about, or have happen to you. Some of the very best illustrations are simple, everyday happenings that all of us as human beings can relate to.

Keep your pen poised and your eye out for:
• Conversations between children
• Stories on television and radio
• News stories
• Material used by other speakers
• Good examples in books and articles
• Catchy phrases, unusual ways of saying something
• Examples from your personal history and that of your friends and family

### Helpful Publications

There are a number of excellent book collections of material for speakers and also several periodicals designed for public speakers.

These are some magazines and newsletters that have proven to be worthwhile.

*Bits and Pieces*
12 Daniel Road
Fairfield, NJ 07006

*Decker Communications Report*
607 North Sherman Avenue
Madison, WI 53704

*Funny Funny World*
8625 Holloway Drive
Los Angeles, CA 90069

*Quote* Magazine
405 Sussex Place
148 International Boulevard
Atlanta, GA 30303

*Sparks from the Anvil*
Concord Industrial Park
Concordville, PA 19331

*Speechwriter's Newsletter*
407 S. Dearborn
Chicago, IL 60605

There are also some organizations that you will find can help you perfect your art as a speaker.

Toastmasters International provides a weekly or biweekly opportunity for members to practice and improve their speaking skills. Most communities of any size have at least one chapter. Here's the address if you want to find out about a club in your area.

World Headquarters of Toastmasters International
2200 N. Grand Avenue
Santa Ana, CA 92711

Two other organizations for speakers are:
The International Platform Association
2564 Berkshire Road
Cleveland Heights, OH 44106

The National Speakers Association
5201 N. 7th Street
Phoenix, AZ 85014

### Setting Up a Quote and Anecdote File

Once your collection of material starts growing, you have to develop an organized method for keeping and finding all those great stories.

Short of storing them by categories in a computer, probably your best bet is to put each anecdote, quote, etc., on an 8½ x 5½ file card with the name of the general topic or category in the upper right-hand corner of each card.

The real secret of good filing is deciding on the appropriate categories—narrow enough to help in locating the material but broad enough so that you don't end up with 1,000 categories.

Place the name of each file category on tab cards and place them in card file boxes on shelves conveniently close to your speech-writing area.

Although speech-writing books have material divided by categories, they won't match your topics. You'll save a lot of time in the long run if you go through the books and put the stories you like in your own file.

### Developing Topical Files

Besides your anecdotes and quotes card file, as a speaker, you will also want to start collecting material in your special areas of interest. This is especially important to you if you are a frequent speaker in your career field or profession.

Get in the habit of saving magazine articles, newspaper clippings, and copies of parts of books. Enlist the help of your friends and colleagues in looking for material in your areas of special interest.

Of course, your local library can be very helpful in researching a particular topic. But don't overlook other local resources that can help you localize a particular issue. These include the local chamber of commerce, charitable institutions, state highway departments, and city officials such as the city manager, police chief, and city clerk.

## LIGHT OPENERS

"I was invited to speak because they wanted something light with no message . . . and I came highly recommended."

"My wife (or husband) told me the other day that now she knows why I'm always asked to speak after dinner. She had just read a doctor's report that said the sense of hearing is considerably dulled by eating, and she decided that was nature's way of protecting people against after-dinner speakers."

"The ladies' (or the men's) room at work has one of those hot-air contraptions for drying your hands. I went in there the other day and someone had neatly written on the button that activates the hot air: 'Press here for a message from the company president'" (or whatever your position is).

"As senator (or whatever), I'm called on to speak quite often. My wife (or husband) says I get up so often that I'm living proof of the old adage that hot air always rises."

"I asked your chairman what I should speak about, and he said: 'About twenty minutes.'"

"My job, as I understand it, is to talk to you. Your job, as I understand it, is to listen. If you finish before I do, just hold up your hand."

"You know _____ is quite a persuasive person. A few months ago she (or he) called to tell me about this wonderful meeting. She said: 'You believe in the goals of our organization, don't you?' I said: 'You know I do.' Then she said: 'You like to share your thoughts with others, right?' I said: 'Sure.' She said: 'And you believe strongly in free speech, don't you?' I said: 'Of course I do.' She said 'Good. How about coming out and giving one?!' So here I am."

"Confucius once said that speaking to an audience of highly intelligent people is like eating soup with chopsticks. It's easier to stir things up than to satisfy the appetite. Today I hope to accomplish both things—to stir up your interest in _____ and to satisfy your appetite for information on the subject."

"I am delighted to be with you today. Now I know a lot of speakers say that, but after struggling with a very austere budget until I've felt like I was wrestling with a 500-pound marshmallow, spending what seemed like a century in federal court, and having to face unexpected financial shortfalls all spring, you just don't know how happy I am to be *here* instead of in my office."

"It's a special privilege to welcome this group of brave people to _____. I say "brave" because I think that anyone who works day in and day out with middle school students (or whatever the group does) must either be brave or crazy, and, of course, I prefer to think of you as brave."

# SPEAKING ENGAGEMENT INFORMATION FORM

Engagement: _____ Occasion: _____

Place: _____ Time: _____ Date: _____

Directions to location: _____



Audience: _____

Appropriate dress: _____

Length of presentation: _____

Topic: _____

Other speakers: _____

Checklist of items to take:

     ____ Reading glasses
     ____ Handkerchiefs
     ____ Throat lozenges
     ____ Notes
     ____ Extra index cards

     ____ Props:


     ____ Audio-visual equipment, supplies:

## ON BEING INVITED BACK
## TO SPEAK TO THE SAME GROUP

"At first I was flattered to be asked back again, but then I remembered that _____ used to be a teacher and was probably going to make me keep doing it 'til I get it right."

"At first I was flattered about being invited back a second time, that is, until my wife (or husband) told me you were probably trying to find out if I'd improved any as a speaker since I was here last."

## ON RESPONDING TO
## A FLATTERING INTRODUCTION

"First, I'd like to ask for a copy of that introduction. Then, the next time anyone asks: 'Who do you think you are?' . . . am I going to have an answer!"

"It's awfully nice to have those things said about a fellow without his family having to go to the trouble and expense of having a funeral."

"Would you mind repeating that introduction? I'd like to tape it so my boss can listen to it."

"That generous introduction reminds me of the man who raised his head up out of the grave on Judgment Day and read the glowing words on his headstone. He shook his head in disbelief and said: 'Either somebody is a terrible liar, or they put me in the wrong hole.'"

## ON BEING HONORED

"This is a moment I wish my parents were here to share. My father would have enjoyed what you so generously said about me. And my mother would have believed it."—Lyndon B. Johnson[1]

"I appreciate your honoring me with this very wonderful occasion. It makes me think of what Jack Benny said once when he was being honored—'I really don't deserve this honor. But then I have arthritis, and I don't deserve that either.'"[2]

# Review

After making a speech one day, Sir Winston Churchill was asked, "Doesn't it thrill you, Mr. Churchill, to know that every time you make a speech, the hall is packed to overflowing?" Churchill replied, "It is quite flattering. But whenever I feel too flattered, I always remember that if—instead of making a political speech—I were being hanged, the crowd would be twice as big."

Then there was Socrates, the first public speaker. They poisoned him.

Those two little anecdotes are just to remind us that there are hazards in being a public speaker. But to minimize them and make sure you don't risk life and limb when you open your mouth, keep the following in mind.

## A DOZEN DON'TS FOR PUBLIC SPEAKERS

1. Don't accept a speaking engagement on short notice unless it's a subject you're thoroughly familiar with and have spoken on before. If you're not given adequate time to prepare, it's better to turn down a request than to leave the audience with the impression that you are an ineffective, ill-prepared speaker.

2. Don't ignore the time and place of the presentation. Find out as much as possible about the setting of your speech. Is it after a meal? Who precedes you?

Who makes the introduction? How is the room arranged?

3. Don't use jokes just because they're funny. A story that interrupts the audience's train of thought does not build rapport; it distracts. Unless the funny story or line helps make a point, it's better to skip it.

4. Don't fail to rehearse. Even if you're a seasoned speaker, you'll do a better job if you take the time to go over your speech from beginning to end several times.

5. Don't try to show them how much you know. The quickest way to lose an audience is to use complex material and data that are difficult to understand and are filled with jargon. Keep it simple. Be sure you're on the same wavelength with your audience.

6. Don't dazzle your audience with a stream of visuals. Visual material used judiciously can help get across your point and focus your audience's attention where you want it. But they can be a decorative distraction if they're done poorly, too many are used, or you're not comfortable with them. Using visuals effectively takes practice.

7. Don't assume you can handle any question if a question and answer period is to follow. Prepare in advance by writing down any question that you think the group might ask and formulate your answer. The person who asked you to speak can also suggest what may be on the minds of the people you'll be addressing.

8. Don't ignore your allotted time. It isn't fair to the audience or to the next speaker. A maximum for the usual type of speech is twenty to twenty-five minutes. If you're asked to speak longer, say an hour, you'll need some type of audience involvement activities.

9. Don't arrive just in time to give your talk. You need to get there in time to get the "lay of the land." Early arrival gives you the opportunity to feel the mood of the audience and a chance to pick up some last bits of information.

10. Don't disregard the makeup of the audience. Make sure your speech is slanted in the direction of the audience's interest, desires, and level of understanding.

11. Don't fail to define clearly the response you want from your audience to what you have to say. You should be able to state your specific objective in one sentence.

12. Don't just "be yourself." While your public speaking should be in keeping with your own style and personality, you have to be more than your usual self. You really can't just speak in a conversational manner and keep your audience's attention. Remember, in a speech situation, you're the whole show, and you have to be livelier and more animated than usual.

# Endnotes

## CHAPTER 1

1. Walt Kelly, "Pogo" comic strip, *The New York Post*, Hall Syndicate, 1970.
2. Max D. Isaacson, speech given February 1, 1980, in Des Moines, IA.
3. *The Sunday Times*, London, October 7, 1973.
4. Jacob M. Braude, *Braude's Handbook of Stories for Toastmasters and Speakers*. (Englewood Cliffs, NJ: Prentice-Hall, Inc., 1957)
5. James C. Humes, *Podium Humor*. (New York: Harper & Row, Publishers, 1975)
6. *7 Biggest Mistakes Business Presenters Make and How to Avoid Them*, booklet published by Decker Communications.
7. "Active Listening," *Quote*, October 7, 1973.
8. Dr. Lyman K. Steil, "Do You Know How to Listen?", *Association Management*, August 1980.
9. Quoted by Isaacson.
10. Ibid.
11. *Nation's Business*, April 1982.
12. *7 Biggest Mistakes . . .*
13. Quoted by Isaacson.
14. Quoted by Scot Morris and Nicolas Charney in, "Stop It! Scaring Off Stage Fright," *Psychology Today*, July 1983.
15. Frank Swiatek in "How to Speak Before a Group," a Learning Dynamics workshop, in San Francisco, February 1984.

16. Quoted by William Safire and Leonard Safir, *Good Advice.* (New York: Times Books, 1982)
17. Dr. Boino Kiveloff, *Prevention Magazine.*
18. Quoted by Dale Carnegie, *The Quick and Easy Way to Effective Speaking.* (New York: Pocket Books, 1962)
19. Ralph Waldo Emerson, *The Conduct of Life.* (South Orange, NJ: Power Publisher, 1860)
20. James C. Humes, *Speaker's Treasury of Anecdotes About the Famous.* (New York: Harper & Row Publishers, 1978)
21. James C. Humes, *Churchill, Speaker of the Century.* (Briarcliff Manor, NY: Stein and Day, 1980)
22. Quoted in *7 Biggest Mistakes . . .*
23. C. H. Spurgeon, quoted by Burton Stevenson, *Home Book of Quotations.* (New York: Dodd, Mead & Co., 1967)

CHAPTER 2

1. "The Act of Listening," *The Royal Bank of Canada Monthly Letter*, January 1979.
2. *Speechwriter's Newsletter*," February 19, 1982.
3. *Quote*, as reported in "Quality Circle Digest."
4. *Effective Business Communications*, Zig Ziglar Corporation.

CHAPTER 3

1. *Effective Business Communications*, Zig Ziglar Corporation.
2. Quoted in *Decker Communications Report*, May/June 1983.
3. Oleda Baker, *How to Renovate Yourself from Head to Toe.* (Garden City, NY: Doubleday & Co., Inc., 1980)
4. Edward J. Hegarty, *How to Talk Your Way to the Top.* (Englewood Cliffs, NJ: Reward Books, 1973)
5. James MacLachlan, "What People Really Think of Fast Talkers," *Psychology Today*, November 1979.
6. Quoted by Dorothy Uris, *Say It Again.* (New York: E. P. Dutton, 1979)

7. Quoted by Jacob M. Braude, *Braude's Handbook of Stories for Toastmasters and Speakers*. (Englewood Cliffs, NJ: Prentice-Hall, Inc., 1957)

8. Dorothy Sarnoff, *Speech Can Change Your Life*. (Garden City, NY: Doubleday & Co., 1970)

9. *Speechwriter's Newsletter*, January 1, 1982.

10. Quoted by Joey Adams, *Joey Adams' Encyclopedia of Humor*. (New York: The Bobbs-Merrill Company, Inc., 1968)

11. John F. Kennedy, Inaugural Address, Washington, DC, January 20, 1961.

12. J. F. Bere, "Second American Revolution," *Vital Speeches*, January 15, 1978.

13. U.S. Circuit Judge Abner J. Mikva in a commencement address at the Chicago-Kent College of Law.

14. Dr. Martin Luther King, Jr., "I Have a Dream," speech in Washington, DC, 1963.

## CHAPTER 4

1. Quoted by James C. Humes, *Podium Humor*. (New York: Harper & Row Publishers, 1975)

2. Bob Orben, "Bridging the Gap with Humor," *Communications Briefings*, November 1983.

3. Quoted by Humes.

4. Quoted by William Safire and Leonard Safir, *Good Advice*. (New York: Times Books, 1982)

5. Quoted by Leonard Spinrad and Thelma Spinrad, *Speaker's Lifetime Library*. (West Nyack, NY: Parker Publishing Co., Inc., 1979)

6. Quoted in *Effective Business Communications*, The Zig Ziglar Corporation.

7. *Effective Business Communications*.

8. Orben.

9. Anonymous, quoted by Dorothy Uris, *Say It Again*. (New York: E. P. Dutton, 1979)

10. Orben.

## CHAPTER 5

1. "3M How-To Guide," 3M Corporation.

2. Louis P. Shannon, *Speaker, Beware! . . . of Platform Pitfalls*. (Newark, DE: Script-Master, 1975)

CHAPTER 6

1. Quoted in *Effective Business Communications*, The Zig Ziglar Corporation.
2. Jacob M. Braude, *Speaker's Encyclopedia*. (Englewood Cliffs, NJ: Prentice-Hall, Inc., 1955)
3. *Oh, God*, screenplay by Larry Gelbart, Warner Brothers, 1977.
4. Allan M. Laing, "Louder and Funnier," quoted by Jacob M. Braude, *Speaker's Desk Book of Quips, Quotes and Anecdotes*. (Englewood Cliffs, NJ: Prentice-Hall, Inc., 1963)

CHAPTER 7

1. Jacob M. Braude, *Speaker's Encyclopedia*. (Englewood Cliffs, NJ: Prentice-Hall, Inc., 1955)
2. Lawrence M. Briggs, *The Master Guide for Speakers*. (Minneapolis: T. S. Denison and Company, 1956)
3. Quoted by Bill Adler, *The Churchill Wit*. (New York: Coward-McCann, Inc., 1965)
4. Lord Leslie Hore, quoted by Jacob M. Braude, *Braude's Handbook for Toastmasters and Speakers*. (Englewood Cliffs, NJ: Prentice-Hall, Inc., 1957)
5. Robert Southey, quoted by William Safire and Leonard Safir, *Good Advice*. (New York: Times Books, 1982)
6. Evan Esar, *20,000 Quips and Quotes*. (Garden City, NY: Doubleday and Co., 1968)
7. Helen Eisenberg and Larry Eisenberg, *The Public Speaker's Handbook of Humor*. (Grand Rapids, MI: Baker Book House, 1967)
8. M. Dale Baughman, *Teacher's Treasury of Stories for Every Occasion*. (Englewood Cliffs, NJ: Prentice-Hall, Inc., 1958)
9. Quoted by William Safire and Leonard Safir, *Good Advice*. (New York: Times Books, 1982)
10. Isaac Asimov, *Isaac Asimov's Treasury of Humor*. (Boston: Houghton-Mifflin Co., 1971)

11. Franklin D. Roosevelt, quoted by Safire and Safir.

12. Braude.

13. Quoted by Herbert V. Prochnow and Herbert V. Prochnow, Jr., *The Public Speaker's Treasure Chest.* (New York: Harper and Row, Publishers, 1964)

14. Quoted by James C. Humes, *Churchill, Speaker of the Century.* (Briarcliff Manor, NY: Stein and Day, 1980)

15. Herbert V. Prochnow, *Toastmaster's Quips and Stories.* (New York: Sterling Publishing Co., 1982)

## CHAPTER 8

1. Jacob M. Braude, *Speaker's Desk Book of Quips, Quotes and Anecdotes.* (Englewood Cliffs, NJ: Prentice-Hall, Inc., 1963)

2. *Communications Briefings*, Volume 1, Number 1.

3. Joey Adams, *Joey Adams' Encyclopedia of Humor.* (New York: The Bobbs-Merrill Company, Inc., 1968)

4. Quoted by James C. Humes, *Churchill, Speaker of the Century.* (Briarcliff Manor, NY: Stein and Day, 1980)

5. Quoted by James C. Humes, *Speaker's Treasury of Anecdotes About the Famous.* (New York: Harper and Row, Publishers, 1978)

## CHAPTER 11

1. Lyndon B. Johnson, on receiving the honorary Doctor of Laws degree from Baylor University, Waco, TX, 1965.

2. *Effective Business Communications*, The Zig Ziglar Corporation.

3. James C. Humes, *Churchill, Speaker of the Century.* (Briarcliff Manor, NY: Stein and Day, 1980)

# Index